Echoes of Krishna
UNVEILING THE SELF THROUGH DIVINE WISDOM

BIBEK SHAH SHANKHAR

Bibek Shah Shankhar

Copyright © 2024 by Bibek Shah Shankhar

All rights reserved.

No portion of this book may be reproduced in any form without written permission from the publisher or author, except as permitted by Canada copyright law.

Contents

About the Author	1
Introduction	3
1. Chapter 1: Dawn in the Dungeon Breaking Free from Inner Chains	5
2. Chapter 2: Playful Wisdom of Vrindavan Rediscovering Joy and Innocence	32
3. Chapter 3: Charioteer's Counsel Navigating Life's Dharma	74
4. Chapter 4: Rukmini's Love Understanding Devotion and Partnership	101
5. Chapter 5: Sudama's Friendship The Riches of Humility and Generosity	121
6. Chapter 6: Dance of the Flute The Art of Subtle Influence	147
7. Chapter 7: Govinda's Guidance Leading with Compassion and Wisdom	168

8. Chapter 8: Battlefield Illumination　　　　　　　　191
   Embracing Life's Challenges

9. Chapter 9: Miracle of the Mountain　　　　　　　221
   Faith and the Power of Protection

10. Chapter 10: Ras Leela:　　　　　　　　　　　　239
    The Dance of Cosmic Love

11. Chapter 11: Maharaja's Maturity　　　　　　　　261
    The Journey from Prince to King

12. Chapter 12: Divine Departure　　　　　　　　　277
    Embracing Endings as New Beginnings

Acknowledgements　　　　　　　　　　　　　　　289

About the Author

Hello, I am Bibek Shah Shankhar, and I warmly welcome you into the world of my creation, "Echoes of Krishna." Born and raised in the culturally rich landscapes of my homeland in Nepal, now living in the bustling city of Toronto, my life has been a journey of bridging worlds–from the tangible to the mystical, the modern to the ancient.

"Echoes of Krishna" goes beyond the boundaries of a traditional book, as it invites readers to immerse themselves in the sights, sounds, and spirituality of Krishna's realm. It is where I pour my heart into exploring the profound wisdom hidden in the lore of Krishna, a figure who has captivated my imagination and spirit since childhood. The scent of incense fills the air, creating an atmosphere of tranquility and devotion. In this book, I invite you to join me on a journey of exploration into the mystical world of spiritual traditions, where every page is like a thread woven into a beautiful tapestry.

In these pages, I blend evocative storytelling with reflective philosophical insights, inviting you to join me on this path of discovery. Together, we will explore ancient wisdom, seeking to connect with something greater than ourselves, to find meaning and enlightenment in our own lives.

Through "Echoes of Krishna," I aim to touch your soul, spark your curiosity, and perhaps offer a new lens through which to view the world. Join me on this transformative journey as we explore a world of wonder, wisdom, and spiritual enlightenment.

Introduction

Welcome to "Echoes of Krishna: Unveiling the Self through Divine Wisdom," a captivating exploration into the life and teachings of Krishna, a revered and mysterious spiritual icon. As the author, I invite you on a transformative journey, where you will immerse yourself in the profound wisdom and timeless teachings of Krishna. These teachings have resonated for centuries and continue to hold relevance in our lives today.

This book is more than just a retelling of ancient stories; it is a rich tapestry, blending philosophy, spirituality, and practical insights drawn from Krishna's life and teachings. Each chapter of this book explores various aspects of Krishna's life, taking us from his joyous days in Vrindavan to his profound teachings in the Bhagavad Gita, showing how these lessons remain significant in today's world.

"Echoes of Krishna" is a book that will guide, befriend, and inspire seekers of spiritual wisdom, lovers of mythological tales, and those searching for deeper meaning in life. This book presents a different angle on how Krishna's teachings can assist us in maneuvering through the challenges of modern-day living, uncovering our genuine purpose, and unleashing our inner abilities.

As we begin this journey, let us embrace the profound wisdom of Krishna, opening our hearts and minds to his timeless teachings that will resonate within us, guiding us towards enlightenment and a life of fulfillment.

Chapter One

Chapter 1: Dawn in the Dungeon

BREAKING FREE FROM INNER CHAINS

In the depths of the somber dungeon, devoid of any light, an overwhelming sense of despair fills the air, suffocating and oppressive. Throughout the ages, the walls have stood firm, their coldness serving as a reminder of the countless seasons that have passed and the suffering endured, their stones etched with the indelible marks of time. Don't mistake this for a regular prison cell; it is far more remarkable than that.

Bound by physical chains and the cruel hand of destiny, Devaki and Vasudeva find themselves trapped within the confining embrace of these ancient walls, anxiously awaiting the arrival of their eighth child. The child, who has been prophesied to be the one who brings about change and acts as a guiding light amid overwhelming darkness. With every passing moment, the anticipation in the air grows denser, stretching each moment into what feels like an eternity as the night deepens.

Despite the bleakness that seems to envelop them, there is an undeniable feeling that something extraordinary is on the verge of happening. The atmosphere feels charged with an undeniable energy, almost as if nature itself is holding its breath, eagerly expecting the arrival of a chosen individual who will bring salvation.

Resting in one corner of the cell is Devaki. Despite the trials she endured during her imprisonment, her face exudes an inner radiance that appears oddly out of place in the dreary surroundings of their enclosure. A personification of quiet strength and unwavering support, Vasudeva occupies the seat beside her. His eyes, which resemble reflective pools of calm, are in stark contrast to the whirlwind of emotions that he is experiencing internally.

Unaware of the incredible miracle about to unfold inside the confines of these stone walls, the guards diligently carry out their duties outside the cell. As the night air envelops them, they are occasionally startled by the distant sounds of the palace, which serves as a stark reminder that there is a world beyond their confinement.

As the grasp of the night weakens and the first rays of dawn appear, a gradual shift can be felt permeating the confines of the cell. It feels as though the approaching dawn is not simply a routine repetition, but a celestial phenomenon that is poised to give a precious gift to the entire world. At this precise moment in time, the dungeon, which is commonly linked with feelings of despair and obscurity, is at the threshold of strengthening into a source of optimism - a sacred realm where the eternal and the fleeting are poised to blend harmoniously.

CHAPTER 1: DAWN IN THE DUNGEON

As the world remains hushed before sunrise, a profound assurance lingers, an assurance that even within the most desolate corners, a beacon of light can emerge, that even within the most unbreakable bonds, the longing for liberation patiently awaits its moment. At this very juncture, our tale begins, weaving together not only the tale of a divine inception but also an account of the invincible spirit that lives within every one of us, patiently waiting to emancipate itself from the confines of our own self-imposed limitations.

Krishna's Birth: Auspicious Signs and Contrast of Environment

With the emergence of the first beams of daylight, casting away the darkness that had shrouded the night, a profound silence fell upon the world, creating an atmosphere of absolute stillness. The profound silence that enveloped the surroundings gave the impression that the entire cosmos was coming together to create a magnificent celestial symphony, as if it were announcing the imminent arrival of a soul touched by divinity. It was at this very moment that Krishna, the eighth avatar of Vishnu, decided to descend into the mortal realm.

With full knowledge of the imminent divine event, the skies adorned themselves in breathtakingly resplendent colors. The stars, in their brilliance, seemed to twinkle with an intensified glow, as if they were engaged in a friendly contest to outdo each other in their efforts to greet the newborn with utmost radiance. The fragrance of heavenly flowers, carried by a gentle breeze, gracefully swept across the land, revealing mysterious whispers of the divine arrival to those who possessed the knowledge to decipher them.

According to ancient legends, celestial beings living in the ethereal realms started a wondrous spectacle by singing hymns of pure joy and heartfelt praise. The voices of these individuals, which were a beautiful mixture of otherworldly sounds, reverberated throughout the universe, filling the atmosphere with a sense of holiness that is rarely experienced on our planet.

The planets, moving gracefully in their celestial dance, formed a rare alignment, almost as if they were paying homage to the newborn. The symbolic meaning behind this alignment was the manifestation of a flawless equilibrium between cosmic energies, a harmonious state that Krishna introduced to the world.

In the realm of our planet, nature appeared to have a personalized way of reacting. The sight was truly extraordinary as flowers defied their typical blooming season, animals displayed unexpected gentleness, and trees moved in a jubilant dance. The entire creation appeared to be in perfect harmony, as if it was actively taking part in this divine event.

In the meantime, the dungeon, with its stark and unyielding nature, stood in stark contrast to the celestial happenings taking place. The walls, with their cold and dampness, stood as a testament to the immense suffering and despair that had been endured within its confines. The lamp inside the room flickered with such inconsistency that it could barely provide any illumination, resulting in a space that was dimly lit and filled with eerie shadows. These shadows, elongated and haunting, served as a reminder of the prolonged presence of darkness that had dominated this place for an extensive period.

Amid this desolate atmosphere, Krishna came into existence, bringing a glimmer of light. The very second he entered this world, a dazzling and radiant light burst forth, illuminating every inch of the cell and forcing the shadows to retreat to the corners. The light that filled the room was not harsh; instead, it was soft, reminiscent of the gentle and comforting glow of the first light of dawn, which delicately rouses the world from its peaceful slumber. Not only was this light a physical entity, but it also carried symbolic weight.

In the presence of Krishna, the air itself felt revitalized and cleansed, as if his mere presence brought a sense of purity. According to the tale, as soon as Krishna shed his first tear, the chains that had held his parents captive mysteriously snapped, as if acknowledging divine energy. The prison cell doors swung open, as if in awe of the incredible feat that had just occurred, silently bearing witness to the miraculous event.

It is said that the moment Krishna cried for the first time, the chains that had imprisoned his parents inexplicably broke free, dropping off as if yielding to the divine energy. As if acknowledging the incredible feat that had just transpired, the locked doors of the prison cell swung open, remaining silent witnesses to the miracle.

Oblivious to the miraculous events happening inside, the guards outside remained in deep slumber, unaffected by the divine intervention unfolding. The intention behind this was to keep the message of the divine arrival hidden, protected, and cherished until the appointed time.

In the presence of this awe-inspiring miracle, Vasudeva's heart swelled with a mixture of love, reverence, and awe. It was in that precise moment that he realized the fact that his son was anything but ordinary.

To Devaki, the birth was not solely the arrival of a savior; it symbolized the culmination of a mother's love and faith. As she looked upon her newborn, a mixture of maternal affection and divine reverence filled her, for she knew her son would embark on a path that would reshape the course of history.

Krishna's birth, which occurred in the confines of a dungeon, held significant symbolism as it embodied the idea of light triumphing over darkness, hope prevailing in times of despair, and liberation found even in captivity. The message aimed to remind us that even during the darkest nights, there is always the assurance of dawn approaching on the horizon. His presence was a stark reminder, underscoring the truth that deep within the core of every being lives a divine spark, bestowed with the power to eliminate the shadows of ignorance and fear.

The Symbolism of Krishna's Birth

The powerful symbolism behind Krishna's birth, occurring within the confines of a dungeon and amidst physical chains and locks, effectively represents the intangible constraints that hold us back on our own personal journeys. Regardless of their intangible nature, these chains are experienced by individuals in various forms.

- **Fear as a Chain**: Similar to how Devaki and Vasudeva were confined by the prison walls, fear has the power to confine us within boundaries that we impose on ourselves. The fear of failure, rejection, or venturing into the unknown can frequently act as obstacles that prevent us from fully realizing our true potential.

- **Doubt as a Restraint**: Doubt, like a shackle, has the power to sabotage our self-belief and hinder our ability to make well-informed decisions. Just as the darkness within a prison cell conceals everything in sight, doubt has the power to obscure our ability to think clearly and make confident decisions, leaving us in a state of uncertainty and hesitation.

- **Insecurity as a Bond**: Insecurity has the power to hold us captive, just as the chains did to Devaki and Vasudeva. When we doubt our worth and abilities, it becomes difficult to fully embrace our true selves and unlock our full potential.

Just like the physical chains that confine prisoners, these internal chains act as obstacles that curtail our freedom and obstruct our path to self-discovery.

The birth of Krishna, occurring within these confinements, serves as a symbolic reminder that liberation from internal limitations is promised.

- **Illuminating the Darkness:** The divine light that accompanies Krishna's arrival signifies the attainment of enlightenment. This thing symbolizes the awakening of consciousness, which has the power to eliminate the darkness that stems from both ignorance and fear.

- **Breaking of Chains:** The symbolic liberation of Devaki and Vasudeva upon the birth of Krishna serves as a powerful reminder that every individual possesses the capacity to emancipate themselves from the figurative restraints they face. The ability to free oneself from internal constraints is a testament to the power of hope, faith, and divine intervention.

- **Opening of doors:** The opening of the prison doors is symbolic of the myriad of new opportunities and paths that become accessible once an individual is liberated from the confines of their own inner prisons. By accepting this invitation, you open yourself up to a vast array of opportunities and the possibility of discovering more about yourself.

- **Divine Intervention and Self-Effort:** The birth of Krishna, encompassing both divine and human aspects, symbolizes the harmonious integration of celestial blessings and individual endeavor in the quest for spiritual liberation. The implication is that although divine energy provides guidance and support; it is ultimately our own efforts that allow us to break free from the internal chains that bind us.

- **Universal Message:** The symbolism of Krishna's birth goes beyond the context of Hindu mythology, reaching a broader significance. This statement resonates deeply with individuals who are actively striving to overcome their personal limitations and unlock their true potential.

- **Embracing One's True Self:** Born as a divine incarnation, Krishna had a clear sense of purpose from the beginning. The birth that took place inside the prison serves as a powerful symbol, representing the profound emergence of one's authentic self despite the many limitations imposed by society and oneself.

Lessons from Krishna's Birth

The birth of Krishna, which defies the physical restrictions of a dungeon, is a strong and meaningful testament to the innate divine potential that lives within every one of us. The focus of this section is to examine the idea that, just like Krishna, each individual carries within them an untapped potential that, once actualized, can overcome any limitation.

- **Inherent Divinity:** Krishna's incarnation as a human with divine attributes mirrors the inherent divinity that lives within every person. Within every person lies an inner divinity that holds boundless potential, profound wisdom, and unparalleled strength. The recognition of this aspect has the power to bring about a transformative effect, granting individuals access to a wellspring of previously unexplored opportunities.

- **Overcoming Limitations**: That Krishna was born in a confined space serves as a powerful symbol of how humans can rise above limitations, whether they are imposed from the outside or come from within. It symbolizes the idea of transcending the boundaries set by society, our upbringing, and even our own self-doubt. The process of transcendence starts by acknowledging and embracing the innate divine nature within oneself.

- **Empowerment through Self-Discovery:** By engaging in this journey of self-discovery, one can experience a profound sense of empowerment. When individuals take the time to understand and fully embrace their inner divinity, they can cultivate a profound sense of purpose, confidence, and direction that permeates every aspect of their lives.

- **Example of Krishna's Life:** Krishna's life is a testament to the power of recognizing and harnessing one's divine potential, as he achieved incredible feats from a young age, serving as an inspiration for others to strive for extraordinary accomplishments and a life of fulfillment.

Despite facing despair, Devaki and Vasudeva's unwavering faith and hope played a crucial role in setting the stage for the miraculous birth of Krishna. The example set by them serves as a valuable lesson on the significance of holding onto faith and hope, especially when faced with the most challenging circumstances.

- **Faith Amidst Despair:** The situation of Devaki and Vasudeva in the dungeon was extremely dire. Despite everything, they held onto their faith, firmly believing that there was something greater at play. The powerful lesson that can be learned from this situation is the importance of having unwavering faith and trust, even in the face of utter despair.

- **Hope as a catalyst:** Their hope was anything but passive; It's a testament to the power of hope as a catalyst for endurance and perseverance. Just as their hope led to the eventual arrival of Krishna, our own hopes can serve as the catalyst for positive outcomes in our lives.

- **Belief in Higher Purposes:** The story of Devaki and Vasudeva serves as a prime example of how people believe in the existence of a higher purpose and a well-structured order in the universe. Sometimes, it is during the most difficult circumstances that we find the potential for profound transformation.

- **Light of Faith and Hope:** The key message of the narrative is that faith and hope act as a beacon of light during dark times, providing guidance and support to individuals as they navigate through challenging circumstances. Just like a beacon that shines brightly amidst a storm, these virtues possess the power to lead individuals towards a future that is filled with brightness and hope.

- **Internal Transformation:** Through its narrative, the story sheds light on the transformative nature of faith and hope, illustrating how they can bring about profound changes within oneself. This transformation goes beyond mere changes in circumstances; it requires a complete shift in how one perceives, approaches, and comprehends life's challenges.

- **Empathy and Compassion:** The importance of compassion and empathy in cultivating hope and faith is emphasized by the actions of Devaki and Vasudeva, who show these qualities despite their personal hardships. The teaching emphasizes the idea that even during difficult times; it is possible for people to tap into their inner resilience and show compassion and empathy.

Personal Growth and Liberation

Identifying Personal Prisons

The concept of personal prisons revolves around the invisible barriers we construct in our own lives, such as limiting beliefs, negative thought patterns, and deep-seated fears, all of which hinder our ability to grow and find happiness. By identifying these prisons, individuals can begin their journey towards personal liberation.

- **Recognizing Limiting Beliefs:** Our potential can be hindered by the limiting beliefs we hold about ourselves and the world, as these assumptions create barriers that prevent us from fully realizing our abilities. One's beliefs can be shaped either during childhood or because of negative experiences. In order to identify these, it is necessary to engage in introspection and be honest with ourselves about our beliefs and the reasons behind them.

- **Understanding Negative Thought Patterns:** When we engage in negative thought patterns, like constantly criticizing ourselves, being pessimistic, or fearing failure, we find ourselves stuck in a never-ending cycle of negativity. It is essential to grasp and acknowledge these patterns for their importance. Cultivating this awareness is possible by practicing mindfulness, which enables us to observe our thoughts with no judgment.

- **Acknowledging Fears:** The power of fear is undeniable,

and perhaps it is one of the strongest forms of imprisonment. The fear of being rejected, failing, or facing the unknown has the power to paralyze us, making it difficult to take risks or explore new opportunities. One important step in conquering our fears is to acknowledge them, rather than trying to avoid or suppress them.

- **Reflection and Journaling:** I wholeheartedly implore readers to dedicate a brief period of time to engage in profound contemplation of their life experiences, as doing so can act as a potent stimulant for personal growth. As a recommendation, I highly advise individuals to make use of journaling as an invaluable tool that can aid them in recognizing and overcoming any personal prisons that might impede their growth. One common question that individuals often ask themselves when they want to identify personal barriers is, "What specific beliefs are currently acting as obstacles to my progress?" or "What fears do I often encounter?" Please take into consideration these options as potential starting points for our exploration.

- **Seeking Feedback:** Sometimes we struggle to acknowledge the invisible boundaries of our own confinement. By seeking honest feedback from trusted friends, family, or mentors, we can gain valuable insights into areas that we may be unaware of.

Steps Towards Freedom

Using Krishna's story as a source of inspiration, individuals can implement practical steps to liberate themselves from internal limitations.

- **Embracing Your Inner Krishna:** Just like Krishna served as a representation of divine potential, it is essential to embrace the notion that you possess an inner divinity as well. The essence of this mindset shift lies in the ability to perceive oneself as both capable and deserving of personal growth and happiness.

- **Challenging Limiting Beliefs:** After identifying the limiting beliefs, it is crucial to take the next step and challenge them head-on. Encourage self-reflection by asking yourself, "Does this belief align with reality?" Is it serving me well?" Make the conscious decision to let go of these limiting beliefs and embrace empowering ones that will fuel your growth and aspirations.

- **Transforming Negative Thought Patterns:** Make a conscious effort to actively transform any negative thought patterns you may have. Various techniques, including cognitive-behavioral therapy (CBT), positive affirmations, and mindfulness, have been effective in achieving positive outcomes. Consider replacing negative thoughts such as "I can't do this" with more positive ones like "I can improve my abilities through practice and determination."

- **Confronting Fears:** It is important to take small steps and gradually confront your fears. Take the first step by starting with smaller challenges, and then gradually work your way up to facing your biggest fears. Examples of stepping out of your comfort zone could range from something as straightforward as voicing your opinion in a meeting to something as complex as embarking on a career change. The more acts of courage you undertake, the more your confidence grows and the less control fear has over you.

- **Learning from Krishna's Compassion:** Take the time to reflect on and internalize the qualities of compassion and empathy that Krishna exemplified, starting with yourself and then extending it to others. Just as Krishna showed compassion towards those around him, self-compassion entails being kind to oneself during moments of failure or difficulty.

- **Incorporating Meditation and Mindfulness:** The act of practicing meditation and mindfulness can allow you to forge a powerful connection with your inner self and tap into the limitless potential that lies within you. The establishment of this unique connection has the power to bring individuals a sense of clarity, peace, and inner strength, equipping them with the tools to overcome internal barriers.

- **Setting and Pursuing Goals:** Krishna's life was driven by a strong sense of purpose. In a similar vein, it is important to establish clear and attainable objectives for your personal endeavors. Your values and aspirations should be in alignment with these goals. In order to make progress, it is important to break down tasks into smaller, manageable steps. It is crucial to acknowledge and celebrate each accomplishment as you move forward.

- **Seeking Wisdom and Guidance:** Seek wisdom from mentors, coaches, or spiritual guides, much like Arjuna sought Krishna's guidance in the Bhagavad Gita. One of the most valuable assets in your journey is the opportunity to learn from the experiences and insights of others.

- **Embracing Change and Uncertainty:** Change and uncertainty were prevalent in Krishna's life, shaping his experiences. Change should be embraced, as it is an integral part of life that provides us with chances for personal development. One important aspect to focus on is the development of flexibility and resilience, which will enable individuals to effectively adapt to various new situations.

- **Creating a Support System:** To enhance your personal growth and motivation, it is crucial to establish a network of individuals who can provide both encouragement and inspiration. To cultivate a positive environment and maximize your potential, it is important to surround yourself with individuals who believe in you.

- **Continuous Learning and Growth:** Throughout his journey, Krishna experienced a constant process of learning and personal growth. Make it a priority to adopt the mindset of a lifelong learner, always seeking new knowledge and growth opportunities. Being receptive to new experiences, ideas, and self-reflection can serve as valuable tools for personal growth.

- **Living with Purpose and Intent:** Following the footsteps of Krishna, make it a priority to live each day with purpose and intent. The act of making conscious choices that align with your highest self and true purpose is what this refers to.

Real-Life Examples: Stories of Transformation

Story 1: Breaking Free from Poverty - The Tale of Maya

In a neighborhood ravaged by poverty, Maya's life was a constant battle against the harsh realities. Just like Krishna's birth in a dungeon, she faced the harsh circumstances of limited access to quality education and resources. Just as Krishna's story depicted physical chains, Maya encountered intangible chains as societal stigma, weighing her down like an invisible burden.

Just as Krishna's story depicted physical chains, Maya encountered intangible chains as societal stigma and what appeared to be a predestined fate. Every day, she lived her life with an unwavering determination to not only survive but to achieve greatness. Maya's journey towards transformation began with a profound realization of her own potential, reminiscent of the radiant light that illuminated Krishna's imprisonment. It was through a computer, generously donated to her local community center, that she embarked on her journey of discovering a passion for Science and Technology.

Maya's journey towards transformation started with a powerful recognition of her own capabilities, much like the divine light that brightened Krishna's confinement. It was through a computer that was generously donated to her local community center that she discovered her passion for Science and Technology.

Despite the challenges she faced, Maya remained undeterred and committed herself to positing knowledge. Through her accomplishment of securing a scholarship to a prestigious university, she showed her ability to overcome the metaphorical chains of poverty. The story of her journey serves as a testament to Krishna's victory over constraining limitations, highlighting the significance of perseverance and unwavering faith in oneself.

Story 2: Overcoming Addiction - The Journey of Alex

Alex's life felt like a prison, with addiction lurking in every corner, dominating every aspect. His true potential remained hidden as he languished in the dungeon of substance abuse.

The addiction that Alex had developed was characterized by a continuous cycle of seeking escape and denying the reality. In a parallel to the prison's darkness that surrounded Krishna's birth, he faced his own inner demons of trauma and insecurity.

The birth of his daughter was a profound and transformative experience for Alex, one that he considered being a divine intervention. Just as the dungeon was illuminated by the light of Krishna's birth, this event became a significant awakening for him. The moment dawned on him that, in order to prioritize the well-being of his child, he had to make some adjustments.

With a deep sense of responsibility as a father, Alex sought support and began his transformative journey towards recovery. Overcoming his addiction and achieving sobriety was no easy feat for him, as he encountered countless obstacles, battled with self-doubt, and resisted many temptations, but his sheer determination and resilience prevailed in the end. The way he transforms is reminiscent of how the chains are broken and the prison doors are opened in Krishna's story, which serves as a powerful symbol of breaking free from the limitations we impose on ourselves.

Story 3: Conquering Fear - Sara's Leap of Faith

Sara, who lived in constant fear and anxiety, felt as if she was trapped in her own personal dungeon. One thing that held her back from growing professionally was her intense fear of public speaking, which she was absolutely terrified of.

The presence of fear in her mind acted as a chain, restricting her from speaking up about her ideas and progressing in her career. Though it lacked physical form, this limitation possessed a reality that was as tangible as the walls that enclosed Krishna's birthplace.

The unexpected opportunity to lead a major project at work was like a shining beacon of hope for Sara in the darkness. The situation demanded that she confront her fear directly and without hesitation.

In her quest for personal growth, Sara sought help through therapy, actively took part in a public speaking group, and dedicated herself to advancing her self-assurance. Just like Krishna's emergence from the dungeon, her first successful presentation was a monumental moment. By breaking free from the chains of fear, she could step into a whole new world full of exciting opportunities.

Story 4: Defeating Despair - John's Victory Over Loss

The trajectory of John's life dramatically changed for the worse after losing his spouse. His sorrow transformed into a prison, a gloomy dungeon filled with despair that appeared to have no way out.

Much like the gloomy and isolated prison where Krishna's life began, John's passage through grief was also marked by darkness and loneliness. Bound by the weight of his sorrow, he found himself unable to break free from the past and make any strides towards the future.

The beginning of John's journey to find light in his darkness involved joining a support group. His moment of awakening occurred when he started sharing his own pain and empathetically listening to the stories of others who had experienced loss and were on the path to recovery.

With passaging time, John gradually came to terms with his grief and, in doing so, discovered fresh ways to pay tribute to his spouse's memory. By establishing a charity under their name, he channeled his personal misfortune into a powerful force for good. The journey that he embarks on is like Krishna's emergence from the dungeon, symbolizing a shift from a state of hopelessness to a life filled with purpose.

Conclusion

In each of these stories, the birth of Krishna is portrayed, and they all serve as a medium to convey profound lessons. Regardless of the personal dungeons we face, whether it is poverty, addiction, fear, or grief, they show that liberation is possible. In the present day, we can see echoes of Krishna's narrative in these transformations, which motivate us to break away from our limitations and fully embrace our true potential.

Guided Meditation Exercise:

- **Finding a Peaceful Space:** The first step is to search for a tranquil and pleasant location where you can ensure minimal interruptions. Find a comfortable spot and either sit or lie down, ensuring that you are in a relaxed position.

- **Deep Breathing:** Take a moment to close your eyes and practice deep, slow breathing for relaxation. As you breathe in, focus on your breath entering through your nose and feel your abdomen rise, then breathe out slowly through your mouth. With every breath you take, let yourself become more and more relaxed and centered.

- **Envisioning Your Prison Cell:** Allow your mind to create a vivid image of yourself being trapped in a symbolic prison cell. Your restricting beliefs, fears, and doubts are all encapsulated within this cell. Please take a moment to contemplate the heaviness of these chains and acknowledge how they have been hindering your progress.

- **The Light of Awareness:** Take a moment to envision a gradual and gentle emergence of a soft light from deep within your being. The light that you are witnessing is a powerful symbol of the inner strength, wisdom, and divine potential that you possess. Observe how the radiant glow emanating from the light source gradually dispels the bleakness and obscurity that shrouds the prison cell.

- **Breaking the Chains:** With each passing moment, as the light becomes brighter, visualize the power of your limiting beliefs weakening and eventually crumbling away. Allow yourself to feel a deep sense of release and freedom as the burdens of these constraints dissolve before your eyes.

- **Opening the Prison Door:** Picture yourself walking purposefully towards the door of your cell, with determination in every step. With every step you take, embrace a growing sense of empowerment and liberation. As you make your way towards the door, you are pleasantly surprised to see it swinging open with ease.

- **Stepping into Freedom:** Leave behind the boundaries of your cell and enter a realm where possibilities are boundless. Allow yourself to fully embrace the feelings of openness, freedom, and lightness that are present. Allow yourself to inhale and embrace this newfound feeling of liberation.

- **Returning to the Present:** Take your time to slowly bring your attention and focus back to the present moment. Begin the process by wiggling your fingers and toes, and then, when you feel prepared, open your eyes.

- **Reflection:** Following the meditation session, allocate some time to introspect and ponder upon the encounter. What did you feel? What limiting beliefs did you break free from?

The practice of this meditation technique has the potential to serve as a powerful tool in visualizing and ultimately experiencing liberation from the constraints of our own personal limitations.

Journal Prompts: Exploring and Overcoming Personal Limitations

- **Identifying Limitations:** What are the 'prison cells' (limiting beliefs or fears) that I have created for myself? How have they affected my life?

- **Understanding Origins**: Where do these limiting beliefs originate from? Can I trace them back to specific events, influences, or teachings in my life?

- **Visualizing Freedom**: What would my life look like if I were free from these limitations? How would I feel, and what would I be doing differently?

- **Learning from Krishna**: How can the lessons from Krishna's birth in a prison inspire me to overcome my personal limitations?

- **Steps Toward Liberation**: What practical steps can I take to break free from these self-imposed chains?

- **Reflecting on Progress**: In what ways have I already made progress in overcoming these limitations? What strengths have I discovered about myself in this process?

- **Future Self:** Write a letter to your future self, describing how you have overcome your limitations and what your life is like now.

The purpose of these journals' prompts is to encourage individuals to engage in profound self-reflection and introspection, ultimately leading them towards a path of self-discovery and liberation, reminiscent of Krishna's spiritual journey.

Embracing the Dawn

As we near the end of this chapter, let us once again immerse ourselves in the profound symbolism surrounding Krishna's birth—a celestial sunrise breaking through the gloom of a dungeon. This narrative transcends being a mere mythological tale; it becomes a captivating legend.

Regardless of the confining nature of our "prisons" filled with fear, doubt, or despair, the birth of Krishna serves as a timeless reminder that a new dawn always awaits, offering hope and renewal. As we witness this dawn, we are reminded of the emergence of hope, a force that fills the air with a renewed sense of possibility.

The story of Krishna, who shattered the walls of a dungeon, serves as a poignant reminder of our own ability to break free from the shackles that bind us. It serves as a reminder for us to tap into the divine power that lives within every one of us and embrace it fully. By accepting and harnessing this inner power, we can break free from the chains that bind us and embark on a transformative journey of self-discovery.

As we meditate upon Krishna's narrative, we should also turn our attention inward and acknowledge the shadows within ourselves that crave enlightenment. Embracing your inner dawn requires acknowledging these areas and shedding light on them. Embracing your inner dawn means acknowledging these areas and shedding light on them, ultimately leading to self-awareness, growth, and gradual liberation.

Just as Krishna's presence marked a turning point in mythology, each stride we take in conquering our personal obstacles signifies the start of a fresh chapter in our individual tales. This invitation offers a chance to embark on a transformative journey of self-discovery, where we can explore the depths of our being and unlock our limitless potential.

Like the pages of a book, your life unfolds with each passing day, revealing opportunities to grow and embrace your true essence. The act of embracing the dawn is not something that happens just once, but an ongoing journey of growth, learning, and transformation.

As we conclude, let us carry forward the spirit of hope and liberation that Krishna's birth symbolizes, allowing it to guide our thoughts and actions. Let's break free from symbolic prisons and embark on personal quests with fearlessness, conviction, and trust in our possibilities. Embrace the dawn within you. It signals a transformative path towards self-discovery and fulfillment.

Embrace the dawn that lies within you, as it signifies the commencement of a transformative journey towards self-discovery, fulfillment, and the ultimate liberation of your authentic self.

Chapter Two

Chapter 2: Playful Wisdom of Vrindavan

REDISCOVERING JOY AND INNOCENCE

Introduction: The Enchanting World of Vrindavan

In the heart of ancient India lies Vrindavan, a place where the ordinary becomes extraordinary. Every stone in this sacred land has a captivating tale, and the air is filled with enchanting echoes of myth and melody. It's important to note that this is not just any location on the map; it's a place filled with history and charm. As we explore the verdant landscapes of Vrindavan, we are captivated by the enchanting tales and profound wisdom of Lord Krishna.

The Lush Forests of Vrindavan

Imagine yourself walking through the enchanting forests of Vrindavan, where the lush greenery surrounds you, and the trees sway rhythmically like dancers in a mesmerizing performance. The lush greenery of the forests not only provides a scenic backdrop for Krishna's childhood but also creates a vibrant and enchanting atmosphere. The tree's branches sway in perfect rhythm with the melodies from his flute, creating a captivating sight, and the leaves shimmer with a joy that evokes memories of childhood.

The Flowing Yamuna River

Meandering through the enchanting town of Vrindavan, the Yamuna River, known for its sacredness and beauty, gracefully enriches the surrounding land with its nurturing and life-giving waters. This river is not just a body of water; it is much more than that. The tranquil ripples and soothing murmurs of the water carry with them narratives of a youthful god, who joyfully played by its edges, took holy plunges, and engaged in enchanting nocturnal dances. The Yamuna river in Vrindavan is not simply a flowing body of water; it carries with it a deep spiritual and historical significance.

The Vibrant Life of the Villagers

In the lively town of Vrindavan, every individual contributes to the divine play of Krishna, making it a pulsating community. Despite the simplicity of their lives, the villagers here are blessed with days that are enriched by the melodious music of devotion and the captivating rhythm of tradition. Far from being ordinary people, the cowherds, milkmaids, and elders of Vrindavan possess a special quality that sets them apart from mere mortals.

While engaged in their daily tasks, both men and women experience a love that surpasses the ordinary, leading their hearts to burst into song. The laughter that fills the air as children play, the chatter of the Gopis (milkmaids) engaging in lively conversations, and the heartfelt songs of devotion that resonate from every home come together to form a beautiful tapestry of communal harmony and pure joy.

A Realm Where the Divine Meets the Mundane

Vrindavan, a place where the divine meets the ordinary, is filled with constant celebration and the echoes of Krishna's flute can still be heard in the hearts of those who live there. The deep-rooted legend and sanctity surrounding this place beckon us to embark on a journey of discovering the profound teachings hidden within the joyful and innocent acts of a god who once roamed the earth as a child.

As we embark on our journey through this chapter, we should fully immerse ourselves in the enchanting spirit of Vrindavan, where we can rediscover those timeless and invaluable lessons that Krishna shared during his joyful childhood. These lessons possess the power to unlock the dormant joy and simplicity that lives every within every one of us.

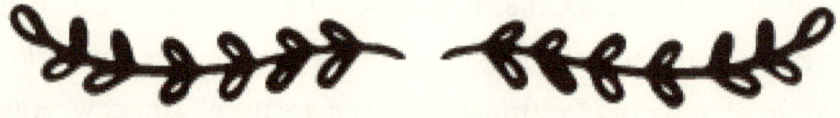

Krishna's Arrival in Vrindavan

A New Beginning: From Darkness to Light

The story of Krishna's journey, which takes him from the confines of a prison to the open and nurturing environment of Vrindavan, is a tale that showcases profound transformation and the divine orchestration at play. The journey that is being referred to in this statement is a powerful representation of moving from a state of darkness to one of light, from being confined to experiencing the freedom of existence, ultimately establishing the foundation for a life that would serve as an inspiring source of hope and happiness for future generations.

In a courageous act, Krishna's father Vasudeva braved the raging waters of the Yamuna river on the night of Krishna's birth, all to rescue him from the clutches of his uncle Kamsa. In a truly remarkable turn of events, Krishna's journey towards a life of freedom and divine play begins with this dramatic escape, which occurred under the cover of darkness and amidst a miraculous parting of the river.

The moment Vasudeva stepped onto the other side, he was met with the beautiful sight of the first light of dawn breaking. When Krishna arrived in Vrindavan, it happened at the same time as the world awakening, which was a significant moment symbolizing the start of a new era, as the first rays of the sun illuminated the darkness of the night.

Symbolically speaking, the shift from a dark and oppressive prison to the lively and life-affirming surroundings of Vrindavan is highly significant. It serves as a representation of the transition from not knowing and feeling fearful to gaining enlightenment and embracing love, from being confined to recognizing and embracing one's true, limitless self.

The village of Vrindavan, which is on the banks of the Yamuna river, is known for its picturesque beauty and the harmonious coexistence of nature and the joyful simplicity of its residents. With Krishna's arrival in this serene and picturesque setting, a golden era began, characterized by the interplay of divinity and humanity.

Vrindavan, adorned with its natural beauty and rustic charm, was reminiscent of a vibrant tapestry. In the lush green forests, where the trees stood tall and proud, there lived a magnificent array of peacocks. These majestic creatures had made these woods their home, and they would often be seen dancing gracefully to the enchanting melodies of nature. As they moved, their vibrant feathers shimmered and sparkled, displaying a breathtaking kaleidoscope of colors. Gently flowing, the Yamuna river, known as a lifeline of the village, nurtures the land and its people with its abundant grace.

In Vrindavan, the villagers embraced a life of simplicity and contentment, finding joy in the little things. The people of the village spent their days engaged in a multitude of activities, including the care of their cows, the cultivation of the land, and observing the customary rituals that were an integral part of their lives. The evenings were filled with a delightful blend of folk songs, dance rhythms, and the captivating tales that showcased their cultural heritage.

Vrindavan was a place where every day was a lively celebration of life, with happiness and festivities all around. The villagers' profound bond with nature and with each other gave rise to a close-knit community that embraced simplicity and found happiness in their unity. When Krishna arrived, with his infectious smile and heart full of love, he brought an extra level of wonder and delight to their lives.

As if he belonged to them, Krishna was embraced by the forests and fields of Vrindavan. As he walked by, the birds would chirp in perfect harmony, almost as if they were performing a symphony in his honor, and the trees, in a display of deep respect, appeared to lower their branches as a sign of reverence, completely enthralled by his playful and divine aura.

For Krishna, Vrindavan held a special place in his heart, far beyond being just a place of refuge. Here, he was not only viewed as a savior who was born with the purpose of liberating the world from tyranny.

With Krishna's presence, Vrindavan underwent a transformation as a new energy enveloped the entire village. The sound of his laughter reverberated through the dense forests and winding lanes, filling the atmosphere with a captivating and enchanting aura. Embracing him as a cherished member of their village, the villagers discovered he was a never-ending wellspring of joy and divine inspiration.

A Microcosm of Divine Play

In the sacred town of Vrindavan, the childhood of Krishna was not merely a sequence of mischievous adventures, but a divine leela (play) that encompassed profound significance and timeless truths. Every single one of his actions, including his playful adventures, held profound symbolism and served as a source of spiritual enlightenment.

This divine play found its perfect backdrop in the mystical town of Vrindavan, where the audience was transported to a realm of spirituality and bliss. The interactions that took place between Krishna and the villagers, the deep bond that he shared with nature, as well as his mischievous yet enlightening acts, all came together harmoniously to form a beautiful tapestry of divine expression.

Through his play, Krishna not only taught the villagers but also spread valuable lessons in love, compassion, bravery, and the joy of living in the rest of the world. The way he lived his life in Vrindavan exemplified the belief that the greatest wisdom can be found in simplicity and joy.

The story of Krishna in Vrindavan, although it is rooted in a specific time and place, continues to captivate people with its timeless appeal. The reminder brings to our attention the universal truths that are embedded in the playful essence of divinity, and it also highlights the immense potential for joy and liberation that exists within every individual.

Krishna's Childhood Exploits

Mischievous Deeds and Playful Antics

CHAPTER 2: PLAYFUL WISDOM OF VRINDAVAN

Krishna's childhood in the enchanting town of Vrindavan was a colorful tapestry woven with countless playful deeds and mischievous adventures, which effortlessly captivated the hearts of every resident fortunate enough to witness them. Despite frequently causing trouble for the villagers, his antics were always filled with an irresistible sense of innocence and joy.

Krishna, who was famously known as the butter thief, had a mischievous reputation. Such was the fame of his affection for butter that mothers in Vrindavan would go to great lengths to keep their butter pots out of his reach, placing them high up and well-hidden. Despite the challenges, Krishna, with the help of his companions and using his clever tactics, would always devise strategies to successfully pilfer the butter. The purpose behind these escapades went beyond mere mischief; there was a greater meaning to them.

One of the most captivating episodes in Krishna's life was when he engaged in a mesmerizing dance with the Gopis, who were the milkmaids living in the holy land of Vrindavan. When the nights were bathed in the soft glow of moonlight, irresistibly enchanted by the captivating melodies emanating from his flute, the Gopis, with hearts filled with longing, would surreptitiously slip away from their homes to unite with Krishna in a celestial dance that overflowed with boundless love and unbridled bliss. The Raas Leela, a dance that holds great significance, transcended mere physical expression.

Krishna was quite mischievous, as evidenced by his many pranks, which included playing tricks on his mother, Yashoda, and startling his friends with sudden appearances and disappearances. Despite their playful nature, these pranks were often vehicles for conveying hidden teachings about love, devotion, and the nature of reality.

The flute of Krishna had an enchanting and mystical quality that captivated all who heard it. Incredibly powerful, the enchantment of these melodies could captivate not just humans, but also animals and even the natural world surrounding them. The flute, which was a symbol of Krishna's connection with the cosmos, served as a powerful tool through which he expressed his divine love and joy.

Despite their appearance as mere child's play, Krishna's playful acts in Vrindavan are actually rich with deeper meanings and spiritual lessons.

One example of Krishna's actions is his stealing of butter, which serves as a symbol for the concept that the allure of divine love and bliss is so powerful that individuals will go to extreme measures to get them. The metaphorical act of stealing butter symbolizes the deep longing of the soul to taste the exquisite sweetness of divine love.

With its portrayal of Krishna's dance with the Gopis, the Raas Leela becomes a powerful spiritual allegory that holds great depth. The longing to unite with the divine is represented by it, as it represents the soul's deepest desires. With their hearts consumed by love for Krishna, every Gopi embodies a distinct soul in pursuit of harmony with the universal consciousness.

The pranks that Krishna plays serve as constant reminders of how important innocence is in one's spiritual journey. According to their teachings, embracing egolessness and childlike simplicity are essential in order to fully experience genuine joy and divinity.

How animals and nature respond to Krishna's flute-playing serves as a powerful symbol, highlighting the universal allure and enchantment of divine melodies. At its essence, the suggestion is that every being is innately connected to the cosmic rhythm, constantly striving to find harmony with the divine.

Yashoda, Krishna's mother, was the focal point of his playful activities, reflecting their loving relationship. By observing these interactions, one can truly appreciate the pure and deep love that exists between a mother and her child, as well as the strong bond between a devotee and the divine.

Lessons from Krishna's Play

The childhood play of Krishna in Vrindavan serves as a powerful lesson, reminding us of the universal nature of joy and love. The message conveyed is that genuine happiness can be found in the little things in life and that everyone, regardless of their social standing or material wealth, has access to divine love.

By consistently defying societal norms, Krishna effectively represented the act of shattering conventional barriers to achieve a state of true spiritual freedom and authenticity.

Understanding Krishna's life requires a deep understanding of the central concept of 'Leela' or divine play. The fundamental lesson it imparts is that life is essentially a divine play, and every individual is an active participant in this grand cosmic dance.

The life of Krishna in Vrindavan showcases an exquisite fusion of the divine and the everyday, creating a truly remarkable integration. The actions of this individual serve as a reminder to all of us that divinity can be discovered in the ordinary aspects of life, and that every moment presents us with a chance to embrace joy and cultivate our spiritual well-being.

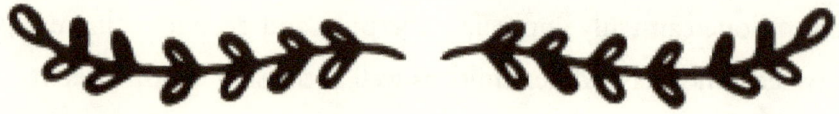

Lessons from Krishna's Play

Rediscovering Joy and Innocence

The narratives of Krishna's childhood in Vrindavan are not limited to mere accounts of divine play; they encompass profound teachings and lessons. Amidst the challenges and intricacies of adulthood, we occasionally find ourselves disconnected from these vital characteristics that define a truly rewarding life.

The time Krishna spent in Vrindavan was filled with immense joy and an effortless inclination towards playful activities. From sunrise to sunset, his days were brimming with laughter, pranks, music, and dance. The unadulterated expression of happiness and spontaneity that we witness in this moment is a powerful reminder of the innocence and purity of childhood, where joy can be discovered in every single moment and even in the smallest of things.

Many of us, as we navigate through the busyness and demands of adulthood, neglect our inner child, the aspect of our being that once found fascination and awe in the world. The invitation presented by Krishna's play encourages us to reestablish a connection with this aspect of ourselves. Encouragement is found in the moments of laughter we discover, the activities that bring us happiness, and the child-like wonder we embrace in life.

The act of participating in play has the remarkable ability to heal and rejuvenate both the mind and body. One benefit of participating in this activity is the potential to reduce stress, improve mental health, and increase creativity. One of the important lessons we can learn from Krishna's life is that integrating play into our daily routine is not just a luxury, but a crucial necessity for our overall well-being.

Many times, innocence is incorrectly perceived as naivety or a sign of weakness. Despite the circumstances, Krishna's life serves as a testament to the fact that innocence can be a powerful and valuable trait. This ability to offer a clear and unbiased perspective on the world creates opportunities for individuals to establish genuine connections with others. The combination of innocence and wisdom can bring about profound insights and a harmonious approach to living.

The Value of Simplicity

In Vrindavan, Krishna's life was a perfect example of living with simplicity. He discovered and then shared his joys with others, which were found in the simplest of things - the beauty of nature, the rhythmic melodies of music, and the comforting warmth of companionship.

Despite being considered a divine incarnation, Krishna preferred to lead a remarkably simple life. He took great pleasure in immersing himself in the beauty of the natural world, deriving immense joy from the companionship of his friends and family, and finding delight in the simple pleasures of indulging in butter and frolicking in the fields.

According to the stories of Krishna, the key lesson is that genuine happiness is not found in material riches or worldly success, but in the ordinary moments and small experiences. Moments such as the joy of a shared meal, the beauty of a sunset, or the laughter of a friend are the ones that truly bring lasting happiness.

When individuals choose to live a simple life, they often find themselves experiencing a greater sense of contentment and tranquility. Decluttering goes beyond tidying up our physical spaces; it also involves clearing our minds and simplifying our lives. The life of Krishna in Vrindavan serves as an inspiration for us to prioritize what is truly important and release ourselves from unnecessary burdens.

One important element of simplicity involves the practice of living in the present moment. Krishna's remarkable capacity to remain completely present, whether he is playing with his friends or immersing himself in the wonders of nature, serves as a valuable lesson in the practice of mindfulness. By teaching us to appreciate the present, it allows us to fully experience and savor the here and now, embracing its beauty and richness.

Inner peace and spiritual growth are often believed to be the result of embracing simplicity, as seen in various spiritual traditions. The life of Krishna serves as a perfect example of this principle. The reason behind his simple lifestyle was not just a coincidence, but a deliberate decision that revealed his profound spiritual understanding.

Although our world is complex and fast-paced, incorporating simplicity into our lives may appear daunting, but it is certainly achievable. To begin, we can take small steps towards improving our lives, such as simplifying our daily routines, practicing gratitude, spending more time in nature, and prioritizing meaningful relationships over material possessions.

The Interplay of Joy, Innocence, and Simplicity

A valuable lesson from Krishna's life is that innocence and ignorance are not the same thing. Despite being wise and discerning, it is possible to hold on to a child-like joy and innocence. The key factor in living a harmonious life is finding and maintaining this balance.

By approaching even the most mundane tasks with a sense of play and creativity, we can find joy in the simplest of activities, such as gardening or cooking. Krishna's lighthearted involvement in day-to-day tasks in Vrindavan is a powerful reminder of the importance of finding happiness in the simple things.

Beyond being a mere place, Vrindavan represented a tight-knit community where simplicity and joy were embraced as the guiding principles of life. By observing Krishna's interactions with the villagers, one can clearly see the positive impact that community life has in promoting and fostering these values. Rediscovering these simple joys can be achieved by building strong, supportive communities in our lives.

The stories depicting Krishna's playful nature and the pure happiness found in Vrindavan resonate with people from all walks of life. Crossing cultural and religious barriers, these experiences speak to anyone in search of a meaningful connection with life's basic delights.

As we take a moment to contemplate and ponder upon the teachings extracted from Krishna's play, let us wholeheartedly embrace and embody the virtues of joy, innocence, and simplicity. The significance of these qualities extends beyond a bygone era; they remain relevant even now. By engaging in activities that allow us to tap into our inner child, finding joy in the little things, and embracing a simpler way of life, we can experience a more fulfilled and meaningful existence.

The Role of Community in Childhood

The early years of Krishna's life in Vrindavan offer a captivating insight into how the community plays a pivotal role in molding a child's upbringing. In the charming and lively village of Vrindavan, every single interaction and every meaningful relationship played a significant role in shaping the colorful tapestry of his childhood, serving as a powerful testament to the profound influence of community in fostering and directing the growth of young individuals.

Krishna among the Villagers

Krishna's engagements with the villagers were notable for a playful and affectionate spirit. He stood out among them as more than just a child; His presence brought a sense of liveliness and celebration to the village.

Krishna played a crucial role in the everyday activities and routines of the people living in Vrindavan. Among his various involvements in the village, he took part in the festivities, enjoyed playing with the cowherd children, and willingly lent a hand to the elders by helping them with small chores. Krishna found great joy in immersing himself in community life, and this also provided him with a meaningful way to establish deep connections with the people of Vrindavan.

Each time Krishna engaged with the villagers, he viewed it as a valuable opportunity for personal growth. Through the medium of playful interactions, he gained knowledge about relationships, empathy, cooperation, and the uncomplicated happiness that stems from connecting with others.

Krishna's play had a deeper significance beyond providing entertainment. Whether he was playing with his friends or helping the villagers, each of his actions contained subtle teachings within them. Through his simple yet profound interactions, he could teach the villagers about the importance of love, trust, and the value of community.

The Villagers' Role in Krishna's Upbringing

Everyone in Vrindavan treated Krishna as if he were their own child. A concept that transcends the nuclear family structure, the villagers collectively took part in his upbringing. Krishna benefited from the collective parenting approach, as it provided them with a nurturing and diverse environment that fostered both growth and learning.

Krishna's character was significantly shaped by the values and traditions of the Vrindavan community. Since he was young, he has been instilled with the values of sharing, caring for nature, and living in harmony.

Krishna received invaluable emotional support and guidance from the community, which made a significant impact on his well-being. The elders of Vrindavan, who were filled with wisdom and had a wealth of experience, graciously provided him with valuable insights and teachings that perfectly complemented his divine nature.

By being a member of a close-knit community, Krishna had the privilege to learn from a multitude of perspectives and experiences. The experience broadened his understanding of life and strengthened his connection with those around him.

The Community as a Learning Environment

Learning in Vrindavan's community was not limited to structured settings alone; it encompassed various informal avenues as well. Krishna's understanding grew as he keenly observed, actively took part, and interacted with the villagers and the natural environment.

The community environment contributed significantly to Krishna's moral and ethical development. The stories, folklores, and daily interactions in Vrindavan were rich sources of lessons in righteousness, bravery, and compassion.

Krishna's upbringing was significantly influenced by the natural surroundings of Vrindavan. The forests, with their towering trees, the winding river, and the diverse wildlife, served as his playground, offering him a valuable education on the interconnectedness of all living beings and the significance of maintaining a harmonious relationship with the natural world.

Within the context of Vrindavan, the tale of Krishna sheds light on the crucial significance of the community in shaping the growth and development of children. This statement shows the positive impact of a nurturing community, which can create a fertile ground for children's learning, growth, and overall development. In today's modern world, this emphasizes the importance of nurturing strong connections within communities, promoting collaborative support networks, and acknowledging the significant influence of the community on shaping the next generation.

Integrating Play in Adult Life

Learning from Krishna's Playfulness

In Vrindavan, Krishna's life served as a remarkable example of how play can hold immense power. Not only was his playful spirit confined to his childhood, but it continued to manifest in his adult years as well.

The key to embracing playfulness lies in developing a certain mindset, rather than simply engaging in particular activities. The concept centers on the idea of embracing life with a sense of openness, curiosity, and joy. For adults, this can imply discovering amusement in everyday scenarios, being receptive to fresh encounters, or merely recognizing the little marvels of existence.

The presence of playfulness within an environment has been shown to foster increased levels of creativity and innovation. Krishna's talent for transforming ordinary situations into playful experiences serves as a reminder that embracing playfulness can stimulate our creativity and enable us to tackle challenges from a new angle.

Making play a part of your everyday life doesn't involve taking part in typical playful activities. There are several ways to make a mundane task more enjoyable, such as turning it into a game, finding joy in the routine, or changing your approach to the task.

The presence of playfulness can have a significant impact on the reduction of stress levels. By engaging in activities that are playful or adopting a mindset that is playful, individuals can effectively reduce the burdens of adult responsibilities, which in turn can have a positive impact on their mental health and overall well-being.

Balance between Seriousness and Play

It is essential to find a middle ground between fulfilling obligations and engaging in recreational activities. Although adulthood often brings responsibilities and difficulties, it is crucial to recognize that prioritizing moments of happiness and leisure is not a mere indulgence, but an essential requirement.

Scheduling dedicated time for play is one practical way to ensure a healthy balance in your life. One way to interpret this is by allocating time for hobbies, engaging in sports activities, or simply relaxing and spending quality time with loved ones. Prioritizing play is essential in a well-rounded adult life.

Infuse a sense of playfulness into your everyday activities. Attempt to be completely engaged and find happiness in every activity you undertake, be it cooking, tending to your garden, or even while you're busy with your work. Engaging in mindful play involves actively taking part, and deriving enjoyment from the experience can be significantly improved and enriched through incorporating playfulness. When you take part in playful activities with your partner, children, or friends, it not only strengthens your bonds but also creates memories that will last a lifetime. This serves to foster a deeper connection and inject happiness and fulfillment into the dynamics of your relationships.

As adults, we often find ourselves in situations where it is necessary to take things seriously. While acknowledging the significance of responsibility, it is equally crucial to understand the value of letting go and embracing the lighter, more enjoyable aspects of life. Krishna's playful nature serves as a reminder that it is perfectly acceptable to release our inhibitions and fully embrace the present moment.

Many people hold the misconception that play hinders productivity, but in reality, it can actually enhance it. By incorporating regular breaks for playful activities or engaging in play before approaching a task, individuals can experience an increase in energy levels and see improvements in focus and performance.

Integrating Play in the Workplace

The establishment of a playful atmosphere in the workplace has been found to correlate with higher levels of job satisfaction, enhanced creativity, and improved teamwork. Making simple changes, such as incorporating playful team-building activities, injecting humor, and fostering a relaxed environment, can have a substantial impact.

The act of encouraging a playful mindset when tackling problems has the potential to result in the development of innovative solutions. When individuals have the freedom to engage in creative thinking and experiment with ideas, their chances of generating innovative solutions increase.

To summarize, integrating play into adult life, similar to how Krishna incorporated it into his own life, is not only helpful but also essential for achieving a well-rounded, imaginative, and blissful existence.

One benefit of this is that it helps in managing stress, enhancing relationships, fostering creativity, and improving overall well-being. The key to leading more enriching lives lies in striking a delicate balance between our responsibilities and indulging in moments of play, enabling us to rekindle the joy and innocence that are often misplaced as we transition into adulthood.

Embracing Spontaneity and Creativity

Krishna's Creative Solutions

Krishna's life, especially during his youth in Vrindavan, was marked by many occurrences that showed his ingenuity and ability to solve problems creatively. These stories are not just entertaining, but they also teach important lessons about thinking creatively.

Among the tales that have garnered the most acclaim, Krishna lifting Govardhan Hill stands out prominently. When the village found itself in a perilous situation because of the relentless downpour brought upon by the god Indra, Krishna, harnessing his divine capabilities, performed an extraordinary act by lifting the entire hill, ensuring the safety and refuge of both the villagers and their livestock. This act showcased not only his immense divine strength but also his ability to think creatively and find a solution to a problem that appeared impossible to overcome.

There is another story that recounts how Krishna, mischievously stole the clothes of the Gopis while they were joyfully bathing in the flowing river. Although it may appear mischievous, the intention behind this act was to impart a lesson on humility and surrender to them. Krishna's unconventional methods were not without purpose, as they often conveyed profound philosophical messages.

The story that depicts Krishna dancing on the head of the serpent, Kaliya, serves as a powerful testament to his remarkable talent for transforming a perilous circumstance into a resounding victory. Rather than resorting to violence, Krishna employed his dancing skills to subdue the serpent, thereby paving the way for its ultimate salvation. The power of creativity is beautifully shown in this story, overshadowing brute force.

Krishna's acts of stealing butter are not merely stories of mischief, but also display his cleverness and resourcefulness. In his many attempts, he would often come up with smart and creative ways to reach the high hanging pots of butter, illustrating the idea that thinking creatively can solve seemingly impossible problems.

Inspiration for Creativity

Taking inspiration from Krishna, we can identify various approaches to nurture spontaneity and creativity in our daily routines. To achieve personal growth, effective problem-solving skills, and a joyful and dynamic life, it is crucial to possess these qualities.

Adopt a playful attitude towards life and approach it with a sense of joy. By adopting a playful mindset, individuals are more likely to engage in experimentation, experience enhanced creative thinking abilities, and find daily routines to be more enjoyable. The essence lies in discovering happiness while engaging in the process of creation and finding solutions to problems.

The key to nurturing creativity lies in pushing yourself out of your comfort zone and wholeheartedly embracing new experiences. By exploring extra activities such as hobbies, trying different routes to work, or experimenting with unfamiliar cuisines, individuals can ignite fresh ideas and gain unique perspectives.

Never lose your curiosity about the world and all that it offers. One way to gain knowledge and deepen understanding is by asking questions, exploring various topics, and seeking to understand different viewpoints. The presence of curiosity serves as a catalyst for creativity, which in turn leads to the emergence of innovative ideas and effective solutions.

Nature, with its vast and diverse landscapes, is a remarkable source that ignites inspiration and fuels creativity. By spending time outdoors, one can not only observe the natural world but also draw inspiration from its immense beauty and intricate complexity.

By being fully present in the moment, you give yourself the opportunity to observe and admire the delicate details of your surroundings, and this heightened awareness can serve as a catalyst for generating innovative thoughts. By clearing the mind, mindfulness opens up space for the cultivation of new thoughts and ideas.

Grant yourself the permission to unleash your creativity without worrying about being judged or failing. Don't forget that creativity is not about achieving a specific outcome, but about engaging in a continuous process, where each attempt made, regardless of the result, contributes to personal growth.

Engaging in artistic activities, such as painting, sculpting, or writing, or simply taking the time to listen to music, can have the wonderful effect of stimulating and enhancing creative thinking. Art and music, both being powerful mediums of communication, go beyond mere forms of expression.

Having an open mind is crucial when tackling problems. Just as Krishna did, it is advisable to seek solutions that may not be immediately clear. It is often through unconventional thinking that we find the best solutions.

Expand your knowledge and understanding by immersing yourself in a diverse range of disciplines, cultures, and schools of thought. Having a diverse range of knowledge and perspectives can contribute to a more abundant collection of ideas and innovative solutions.

By engaging in regular reflection and journaling, individuals can effectively merge their thoughts and ideas, resulting in improved clarity of thinking and the emergence of creative insights.

When trying to come up with ideas, it's helpful to practice brainstorming and free association techniques. Give yourself the freedom to let your mind wander and delve into various possibilities with no limitations.

The act of collaborating with others has the potential to bring in a range of perspectives and ideas, thereby boosting creativity. One of the most effective ways to stimulate creativity is by organizing group discussions and brainstorming sessions, as these provide ground grounds for new ideas to flourish.

The Balance of Creativity and Practicality

It is crucial to balance embracing creativity and spontaneity and practicing practicality and discernment. Krishna, known for his creative nature, consistently showed purposeful actions that were always in alignment with a greater good.

Don't limit your creative thinking to only major projects or problems; incorporate it into your everyday decisions and tasks as well. By implementing this practice into your everyday life, you can experience a greater sense of fulfillment and find your days more interesting.

One of the key aspects of creating a successful work environment is to actively promoting and support a culture of innovation and creative thinking. Create a nurturing atmosphere that not only welcomes but also actively encourages the exploration and implementation of innovative concepts.

In situations where you are confronted with obstacles, attempt to avoid relying on conventional methods and instead, embrace a more creative mindset. By employing a creative approach, one can transform challenges into valuable opportunities.

In summary, the act of embracing spontaneity and creativity, as exemplified by Krishna, has the potential to transform one's life into a more enriching and vibrant experience. By attempting to integrate these qualities into our everyday routines and approaches, we can improve our problem-solving abilities, add value to both our personal and professional lives, and sustain a feeling of happiness and awe in everything we undertake. The life of Krishna stands as a testament, reminding us that creativity and spontaneity should not be confined to the arts or sporadic occasions, but they should be integral parts of a life well-lived.

Krishna's Flute: A Symbol of Divine Music

The flute of Krishna, which is a simple yet profound symbol in the tales of Vrindavan, holds a special place in the lore that surrounds his life. It's not just an instrument; it's a symbol of divine music that resonated with the essence of joy and spiritual upliftment. Let's explore the magic of Krishna's flute and how music, in its universal language, can be a source of joy and spiritual nourishment in our lives.

The Magic of Krishna's Flute

The flute in Krishna's hands transcended being a mere musical instrument, becoming an enchanting source of melodies in the sacred land of Vrindavan. With its enchanting melodies, the instrument could transport individuals beyond the realm of ordinary existence, granting a profound serenity and joy to anyone fortunate enough to encounter its harmonies.

Not only did Krishna's flute influence human listeners, but it also affected other beings. According to legend, when Krishna played, not only did the people of Vrindavan come to a halt, completely entranced, but the animals and even the natural elements themselves seemed to react. The divine music had such a captivating effect that cows would pause their grazing, birds would perch silently, and even rivers would slow their flow.

The enchanting sound of Krishna's flute resonated with such beauty and grace, as if it were a divine call that deeply touched the depths of one's soul. The invitation represented something more than just a physical experience; it was a glimpse into a world beyond our senses, a gentle reminder of the divine presence that exists in everything. The music of Krishna's flute served as a gateway for the inhabitants of Vrindavan, allowing them to delve into a realm of deeper joy and forge a stronger connection with the divine.

The flute, essentially, and fundamentally, represented a form of divine communication. The music was not just sound; it was a language that addressed to the heart, transcending words and conventional forms of communication.

Music as a Medium of Joy

Just like the divine melody of Krishna's flute, music has the extraordinary power to bridge the gap between different cultures and languages, making it a universal language. One of its remarkable abilities is to express and evoke emotions in ways that words frequently cannot accomplish.

Just like the spiritually transformative impact of Krishna's flute, music has the power to elevate and uplift our souls. It has the potential to serve as a means for meditation, relaxation, and spiritual exploration.

There have been multiple studies conducted that have showed the therapeutic benefits of music. Engaging in this activity has the potential to reduce stress levels significantly, alleviate feelings of anxiety, and contribute to an overall improvement in mental well-being. The ability of music to calm us is evidence of its powerful influence in creating harmony within ourselves.

The act of integrating music into our daily lives has the potential to bring us both joy and comfort. There are various ways to relax and unwind, such as listening to calming melodies, singing your favorite songs, or even taking up the challenge of learning to play a musical instrument. Music possesses an unparalleled power to convert the ordinary aspects of life into extraordinary and enchanting experiences.

Not only is music a form of cultural expression, but it also serves as a powerful medium for artistic expression. Just as the various expressions of joy and devotion found in Vrindavan mirror the diversity of human experiences and traditions, so too does it reflect the same diversity.

Through its captivating melodies and harmonies, music possesses the remarkable capability to bring people together, forging a strong sense of community and shared experiences. Engaging in group musical activities, such as singing or dancing together, has the potential to cultivate strong connections among individuals and instill a deep sense of belonging.

Lessons from Krishna's Flute

The flute played by Krishna, which is a humble bamboo instrument, serves as a profound lesson on the strength and beauty found in simplicity. This shows that even the simplest things can hold joy and beauty, highlighting that true artistry is not solely dependent on the tool, but on the expression.

The divine music that emanated from Krishna's flute served as a mirror, reflecting his inner beauty and divinity. One lesson it imparts is the idea that genuine expression originates from within ourselves and highlights the fact that each individual possesses a distinct 'melody' to contribute to the world.

The symbolic response of nature to Krishna's flute-playing serves as a profound representation of the inherent connection and seamless harmony that exists between music and the natural world. This serves as a reminder of how crucial it is for us to live in harmony with nature and the environment, acknowledging their significance.

Alongside their captivating nature, the captivating melodies emitted by Krishna's flute are also used to engage in meditation and self-reflection. By serving as a pathway, music enables us to explore the depths of our inner world and provides a sacred space for introspection and contemplation.

The joy that the people of Vrindavan experience when Krishna plays his flute emphasizes the happiness that can be found in communal musical moments. This shows how music can serve as a collective journey, strengthening our connections with others.

The enchanting sound of Krishna's flute serves as a source of inspiration, motivating us to follow our artistic inclinations. Engaging in various forms of art, such as music, painting, writing, or any other creative outlet, can be a source of great happiness and fulfillment.

To conclude, it is important to note that the story of Krishna's flute in Vrindavan is not merely a mythological narrative. Embracing music in our lives, whether in the role of listeners, performers, or creators, not only encourages us but also allows us to delve into the profound connection it establishes with our inner beings and the external world. Allow the enchanting melodies of Krishna's flute to serve as a constant reminder of the profound impact that music, with its inherent beauty, simplicity, and transformative power, has on our lives.

Reconnecting with Nature

The deep bond that Krishna shares with nature, as demonstrated through his life in Vrindavan, serves as a profound reminder of the profound connection we can establish with the natural world. In this section, we delve into the exploration of Krishna's relationship with nature, examining how it can serve as an inspiration for us to reestablish our connection with the environment and adopt a lifestyle that is both conscious and sustainable.

Krishna's Connection with Nature

The life of Krishna in Vrindavan was like a mesmerizing symphony, where he lived in perfect harmony with nature. Throughout his childhood, there were countless instances that showcased his profound bond with not only the trees and the river Yamuna, but also with the animals and the entire ecosystem of the village.

The forests of Vrindavan played a significant role in Krishna's adventures, going beyond being mere backdrops; He would often be seen playing his flute under the Kadamba trees, or herding cattle through the lush groves. His divine presence filled these forests with life, and it is believed that the trees would even respond to his playful actions.

Another important aspect of Krishna's life was the Yamuna River. It was not only a source of water, but also served other purposes. The river, which is frequently portrayed as a witness to his divine activities, not only symbolizes his greatness, but also serves as a reminder of the purity of nature because of its clean and nurturing waters.

The way Krishna interacts with animals, specifically the cows of Vrindavan, demonstrates his deep understanding and affection for every living being. Many people often depict him as a compassionate caretaker of the cows, and his deep connection with them serves as a symbol for the profound bond that can be formed between humans and animals.

Vrindavan's ecosystem, with its diverse range of elements such as peacocks, parrots, flowering plants, and fruit-bearing trees, all contributed in some way to enrich Krishna's life. The ideal of living in harmony with nature is beautifully exemplified by the interdependence between Krishna and his natural surroundings.

Lessons on Environmental Consciousness

One of the valuable lessons that Krishna's life teaches us is the importance of having respect for all forms of life. His compassionate interactions with animals and plants serve as reminders that every creature and element in nature possesses its own unique role and significance.

The untouched and pure surroundings of Vrindavan in Krishna's era serve as a powerful reminder of the importance of adopting sustainable practices in our modern world. Taking steps to preserve our natural environment, responsibly using resources, and ensuring the protection of ecosystems are essential actions that play a vital role in maintaining the delicate balance of nature.

It is important to approach the act of engaging with nature with both mindfulness and reverence. By taking simple actions like planting trees, conserving water, and reducing pollution, we can make significant strides in nurturing the environment.

Much like Krishna, who found both joy and spiritual fulfillment in nature, we can also find peace and inspiration by connecting with the natural environment. By spending time in natural settings, we can reconnect with ourselves and the larger world that surrounds us.

Of the most important things we can do is to teach children how to appreciate and care for the environment. By showcasing Krishna's playful yet respectful interaction with nature, we can effectively educate future generations about the significance of environmental stewardship.

In the same way that the community of Vrindavan played a significant role in Krishna's upbringing, community efforts are crucial for the preservation of the environment. Engaging in collective actions, such as participating in community gardening, organizing cleanup drives, and supporting wildlife conservation initiatives, can have a meaningful impact.

The healing properties of nature are inherent and can have a profound effect on both physical and mental health. By engaging in activities such as gardening, hiking, or just immersing oneself in green spaces, individuals can enhance their overall health and well-being.

Nature plays a significant role in many cultural and spiritual practices. By recognizing and showing respect for the cultural and spiritual significance of natural sites, individuals can develop a deeper appreciation and sense of responsibility towards the preservation and conservation of these areas.

The life of Krishna serves as a source of inspiration for us, motivating us to become powerful advocates for the environment. The importance of supporting policies and initiatives that prioritize the protection of natural habitats, conservation of resources, and promotion of sustainable development cannot be overstated in today's world.

To conclude, Krishna's profound bond with nature serves as an inspiring testament to humans' potential for peacefully coexisting with the natural world. By reflecting on the experiences and teachings of his life, we can cultivate a more profound sense of environmental awareness, acknowledge the interconnectedness of all living beings, and actively engage in the preservation of our natural environment. By incorporating nature into our daily lives, we not only contribute to the well-being of the environment but also experience a profound sense of peace, fulfillment, and connection with the world, ultimately enhancing our own lives.

The Joys of Friendship

The life of Krishna in Vrindavan provides valuable lessons that transcend time, teaching us about the immense happiness found in friendships and the significance of nurturing authentic connections. In Vrindavan, his interactions with friends and companions were characterized by pure love, joy, and mutual respect, which served as perfect examples of what ideal friendships should be.

Krishna's Friendships in Vrindavan

The friendships that Krishna nurtured and developed in Vrindavan were based on a deep sense of unconditional love and a mutual respect for one another. Countless adventures were shared by him with his closest friends, the cowherd boys (Sakhas), which included herding cattle and exploring the forests. The relationships that existed were completely devoid of any societal hierarchies or materialistic expectations; they were solely built on camaraderie and love.

Among the many stories of friendship, one that stands out is the tale of Krishna and Sudama. Although Krishna belonged to the royal class and Sudama came from a humble background, their friendship remained unaffected by the societal divisions. The story, in which Krishna gives a warm welcome to his childhood friend Sudama and gives honors upon him, serves as a testament to the profound depth and genuine sincerity of their friendship.

Krishna's mesmerizing flute-playing had a magical effect, attracting his friends towards him and creating beautiful moments filled with collective joy and unity. The melody played by the flute was a beautiful and enchanting call, inviting everyone to come together and share in the delightful moments of life.

Krishna and his group of friend's experienced moments of pure joy that were both simple and profound, ranging from engaging in playful games to sharing meals together. Even though these moments may appear ordinary at first glance, they are filled with a strong sense of unity and joy that we all experience together.

The Importance of Meaningful Relationships

One benefit of having meaningful friendships is that they can provide emotional support, which is crucial for our well-being, as well as a sense of belonging. The organization provides a secure and welcoming environment where individuals can freely express their happiness, sadness, and all the various moments that make up life. Much like Krishna and his companions, who stood by each other, our friendships can provide us with the strength and comfort we seek.

Friendships encompass more than just companionship; Healthy friendships challenge us, inspire us, and help us grow. They provide us with encouragement to improve ourselves, similar to the uplifting nature of Krishna's friendships.

In a world that is becoming more and more isolated, the importance of authentic connections cannot be emphasized enough. Krishna's life serves as a powerful example, demonstrating the significance of cultivating meaningful relationships with the people in our lives. This serves as a reminder that genuine happiness is often found in the moments we share with others.

In today's era, dominated by social media and short-lived connections, Krishna's friendships serve as a reminder for us to move beyond surface-level interactions and prioritize the cultivation of profound and significant relationships.

One of the valuable lessons that friendships offer is the ability to develop empathy and understanding. By surrounding himself with a diverse group of friends, Krishna exemplifies the idea that embracing different perspectives and backgrounds can enrich our understanding and overall experience of the world.

The interactions that Krishna has with his friends in Vrindavan serve as a powerful reminder of the significance of community and the well-being of the collective. The deep sense of belonging and the mutual care that exists within a community can have a significant and lasting effect on the happiness of both individuals and the collective.

In the realm of spirituality, friendships are often considered being sacred entities. These bonds are not merely social constructs, but they also hold a spiritual significance as they assist us in our personal quest for self-discovery and fulfillment.

Just like any other type of relationship, friendships also demand effort and nurturing to flourish. The key elements for successful relationships include mutual respect, understanding, and the dedication to invest time and energy. Maintaining enduring friendships in Vrindavan was of utmost importance to Krishna, and he ensured this through constant nurturing and mutual affection.

Ultimately, the friendships established by Krishna in Vrindavan offer a profound understanding of what it means to be a loyal friend - a bond rooted in unconditional love, reciprocal respect, and shared moments of bliss. These friendships rise above the norm, granting us glimpses into the boundless potential of human connections. When we invest time and effort in developing and valuing deep connections with others, we open ourselves up to the immense happiness and satisfaction that can only be found in genuine companionship.

Conclusion: Embracing the Wisdom of Krishna's Childhood

Summarizing the Lessons

One can learn a lot about the significance of joy and play by looking at Krishna's life in Vrindavan. By demonstrating playful antics and maintaining a joyful disposition, he reminds us of the importance of cherishing the simple joys in life and approaching our daily tasks with a light-hearted spirit.

Krishna's interactions and lifestyle serve as profound lessons because of the clear innocence and simplicity. They invite us, urging us to not only appreciate the beauty found in simplicity, but also to approach life with a heart that is open and pure.

In Vrindavan, the birthplace of Krishna, the profound sense of community underscores the crucial role of cultivating robust relationships and offering unwavering support to our fellow beings. The recognition of the value of collective well-being and shared experiences underscores their importance.

Krishna's ability to think creatively and approach situations in unique ways inspires us to think creatively and find innovative solutions to our own challenges.

The enchanting melodies emanating from Krishna's flute, which resonated throughout Vrindavan, not only brought harmony and joy to all who heard them, but also imparted a profound lesson about the transformative influence of music and art in enhancing our existence and fostering connections with those around us.

The deep affinity that Krishna shares with nature prompts us to reflect on the significance of nurturing and conserving our natural surroundings. The encouragement to embrace a lifestyle that respects and nurtures the planet is something that deeply resonates with us.

The friendships that Krishna established, which were built on the foundation of unconditional love and joy, serve as a valuable lesson for us on the importance of cultivating profound and meaningful connections in our own lives.

Rediscover Your Own 'Vrindavan'

Let us attempt to assimilate the valuable lessons from Krishna's childhood into our own lives. By exploring each aspect of Krishna's life in Vrindavan, we can uncover a path towards rediscovering our own state of joy, simplicity, and innocence.

Explore strategies to integrate moments of play and delight into your daily rituals. Whether it's engaging in hobbies, sharing laughter with loved ones, or finding joy in the simplest of things, grant yourself the freedom to fully embrace and experience happiness.

By simplifying your life, you can also simplify your mindset. Take a cue from children and embrace innocence by viewing the world with wonder and openness.

Take steps to enhance your sense of community, which will cause a greater feeling of belonging and connectedness. Encourage interaction with those in your vicinity, extending support, and actively taking part in group activities that promote a sense of unity.

Open your mind to new ideas and be innovative in your thinking and approach. Embrace the various forms of creativity and harness them as a valuable resource for problem-solving and self-expression.

Include music and art in your life, allowing them to enhance your experiences and bring joy. Regardless of whether you are actively involved in the process of creation or simply taking the time to appreciate, it is crucial to let these different forms bring a sense of harmony and joy into your life.

By allocating quality time to immerse yourself in the beauty of nature, and simultaneously adopting sustainable practices, you can experience a more fulfilling and environmentally conscious way of living. Allow yourself to be inspired and rejuvenated by the beauty of the natural world.

By dedicating time and energy to your friendships and relationships, you can strengthen and deepen those connections. Seek to build connections that are rooted in mutual respect, love, and joy.

By integrating these elements into our daily routines, we can establish our own personal 'Vrindavan' - a sacred place filled with happiness, simplicity, and purity, where every aspect of our existence reflects the teachings derived from Krishna's early years. Together, let us embrace these timeless teachings and allow them to be our compass as we navigate through life in search of fulfillment and happiness.

Chapter Three

Chapter 3: Charioteer's Counsel

Navigating Life's Dharma

Introduction: The Battlefield of Kurukshetra

The epic Mahabharata harbors a remarkable dialogue that has transcended the constraints of time and space, perpetually igniting the hearts and minds of countless seekers as they embark upon their transformative spiritual odyssey. The Bhagavad Gita, which is a dialogue, takes place on the sacred plains of Kurukshetra, a land that holds immense historical and spiritual importance.

The Bhagavad Gita: A Divine Discourse

The Bhagavad Gita, which comprises 700 verses, is a significant Hindu scripture and is included in the Indian epic Mahabharata. In this text, the conversation takes place between Prince Arjuna and his charioteer, Lord Krishna, who is revered as an incarnation of the divine. The profound and enlightening philosophical and spiritual discourse contained within this sacred text tackles the essential inquiries about life, duty, and righteousness.

In the background of this sacred conversation lies the battlefield of Kurukshetra, where two mighty armies are prepared for battle. The Pandavas, who have been wronged by their kin, are positioned on one side, while their cousins and rivals for the throne, the Kauravas, are positioned on the other side. The approaching battle is not merely a physical encounter, but a moral and ethical dilemma that embodies the everlasting struggle between good and evil.

Arjuna's Dilemma: The Warrior in Conflict

Standing in his chariot, Arjuna, a skilled and honorable warrior, finds himself at the center of this narrative, grappling with doubt and moral confusion. When he gazes across the vast expanse of the battlefield, he is not just met with the sight of adversaries, but also with the presence of teachers, friends, and even family members who stand on both sides. The thought of battling against his own relatives causes his heart to waver, creating a complex inner conflict.

Krishna's Role: The Divine Charioteer

As the crisis unfolds, Krishna takes on the dual role of Arjuna's charioteer and spiritual mentor, providing guidance and support. During the battlefield, a remarkable transformation occurs, turning it into an unexpected classroom of higher learning where Krishna imparts teachings that go beyond the immediate context of the war.

The counsel he provides encompasses the fundamental aspects of life, duty, and the journey towards spiritual liberation.

Symbolism of the Battlefield

The battlefield of Kurukshetra serves as a powerful symbol of the complex human condition, wherein individuals find themselves trapped amidst the chaos and turmoil caused by conflicting duties, overwhelming emotions, and challenging moral dilemmas. The representation of the inner struggle that every individual experiences is a depiction of the conflict between our higher and lower selves, the battle between our spiritual aspirations and our worldly desires.

The Eternal Relevance of the Gita

Although the teachings of the Bhagavad Gita are rooted in a specific historical and cultural context, they possess universal relevance. The relevance of its exploration of duty (dharma), righteousness (adharma), and the journey towards self-realization transcends time, making it as pertinent today as it was thousands of years ago. By offering a timeless roadmap, this resource assists us in navigating the intricacies of life, enabling us to make choices that are in harmony with our most profound truths and values.

The Bhagavad Gita, a sacred text, delves deep into the moral and emotional dilemma of Arjuna, a prominent character, who grapples with internal conflict amidst the chaos of the battlefield of Kurukshetra, symbolizing the timeless struggle that all humans face when confronted with challenging decisions. The following section takes a comprehensive dive into Arjuna's crisis, meticulously unraveling the intricate layers of his internal struggle and shedding light on the profound implications it has for the entire community.

The Dilemma of Arjuna

As the great battle of Kurukshetra is about to begin, Arjuna, positioned in his chariot, displays his readiness and expertise as a skilled warrior. However, as he carefully surveys the vast and chaotic battlefield before him, his keen eyes can discern the faces of not only his formidable opponents, but also those of his dear relatives, respected teachers, and revered elders. The act of receiving this recognition deeply affects him, causing a moral and emotional crisis to arise within him.

The major dilemma that Arjuna faces revolves around his duty as a warrior, which compels him to fight in the war, and his profound affection and compassion for his relatives, who denounce any act of violence directed towards them. This conflict is more than just a personal predicament; it is universal that symbolizes the inherent contradictions between human responsibilities and feelings.

Arjuna, being deeply conscious of the potential outcomes of the war, understands the inescapable loss of lives, the devastating impact it would have on families, and the moral burden of taking the lives of his own relatives. The triumph experienced in a war like this feels devoid of meaning, burdened with sadness and a sense of culpability.

The crisis that Arjuna is facing has its origins deeply embedded in the fundamental principles of morality and ethics. The situation raises several thought-provoking questions regarding what defines right action, the ethics behind justifying war, and the moral consequences of fulfilling duty despite conflicting personal values.

Krishna's Role: The Divine Guide

In this moment of deep confusion and overwhelming despair, Krishna, who takes on the role of Arjuna's charioteer, steps into the position of a spiritual mentor and guide. The counsel that he provides to Arjuna goes beyond the immediate context of the war and instead offers timeless wisdom on various aspects of life, including duty and spirituality.

The guidance provided by Krishna extends beyond the mere strategies employed in war. Through his exploration of the underlying spiritual and ethical dilemmas that Arjuna grapples with, he transforms the discussion from a simple discourse on warfare into a profound and thought-provoking dialogue on the principles that govern our existence and moral compass.

By employing the setting of the battlefield and highlighting Arjuna's predicament, Krishna skillfully conveys the intricate and nuanced nature of life's obligations and decision-making processes. In his explanation, he clarifies the concept that life is frequently characterized by conflicting obligations and opposing forces, causing the use of wisdom and discernment to navigate through them.

By studying Krishna's teachings, we come to realize the expansive cosmic perspective that lies beyond. Through his explanation of the fleeting nature of existence and the everlasting essence of the soul (Atman), he equips Arjuna with a wider context to grasp his obligations and the temporary nature of earthly dilemmas.

Understanding Dharma and Righteous Action

Dharma, the righteous duty, is thoroughly explored and understood through the insightful teachings of Krishna. In his emphasis, he highlights the uniqueness of Dharma for every individual, which is shaped by their societal role, personal skills, and life circumstances.

In his teachings, Krishna emphasizes the difference between general dharma and svadharma, which is the individual's specific duty. In his advice to Arjuna, he emphasizes the importance of staying true to one's svadharma, even in the face of difficulties, because each individual has a distinct path to righteousness.

One of the key elements of Krishna's advice is the concept of 'Nishkama Karma', which emphasizes the importance of taking action without being attached to the outcomes. The advice given by him to Arjuna is to carry out his duties as a warrior without getting attached to the outcome, be it victory or defeat, success or failure.

The Universality of Arjuna's Crisis

The situation that Arjuna found himself in on the battlefield can be viewed as a symbolic reflection of the broader human experience. In their lives, every person encounters conflicting choices that involve their duty, moral values, and personal relationships.

Through Arjuna's predicament, the Gita delves into the complexities of ethical decision-making, offering valuable insights. The focus is on the value of self-examination, recognizing one's obligations, and selecting actions that are consistent with a superior moral and spiritual structure.

The transformation of Arjuna, who was initially confused and faced with moral dilemmas, into a person of clarity and decisive action with the guidance of Krishna, serves as a powerful symbol representing the path of self-realization and spiritual awakening.

In summary, the narrative of Arjuna's dilemma and Krishna's guidance in the Bhagavad Gita offers wisdom that surpasses its ancient origins, providing valuable lessons for tackling moral and ethical challenges in any era. The act of introspection serves as an encouragement, interesting us to gain a deeper understanding of our individual roles and responsibilities (svadharma), which in turn guides us towards making decisions that are in harmony with righteousness and the greater cosmic truth. Even in the present day, the wisdom that was imparted on the battlefield continues to hold significance, serving as a guiding force in our journey towards ethical living and spiritual fulfillment, just as it did in the times of Arjuna.

Understanding Dharma

Introduction to Dharma

In the Bhagavad Gita, a text that holds great significance, one of the key teachings that stands out is the profound concept of Dharma, which embodies the quintessence of duty and morality. It encompasses a set of principles that include duty, righteousness, and moral responsibility. Krishna introduces the concept to Arjuna in order to help him navigate and resolve the moral dilemma he is facing on the battlefield of Kurukshetra.

The concept of Dharma is neither static nor singular. The extent of this difference is not fixed and is subject to the individual, considering their societal role, personal capabilities, and specific circumstances. In his exposition of Dharma, Krishna offers not only a personal guide for Arjuna, but also a universal principle that holds relevance for all of humanity.

Duty and Righteousness

The Dharma of every person is distinct, and it is shaped by their societal position, inherent nature, and the specific stage of life they are in. Arjuna, being a Kshatriya, has a responsibility to maintain justice and righteousness, even in situations where making tough decisions is necessary.

According to Krishna, the concept of adhering to one's Dharma goes beyond simply fulfilling one's responsibilities; it also encompasses the importance of carrying out these duties with ethical considerations in mind. The adherence to Dharma, which is the moral and ethical duty, is of utmost importance as it plays a vital role in upholding both social and cosmic harmony.

Arjuna's hesitation to take part in the battle signifies a clash of moral obligations, known as Dharma. A tough decision lies before him as he finds himself torn between his obligation as a warrior and his ethical reservations about inflicting harm on his own kin. The primary aim of Krishna's guidance is to find a resolution to this conflict by offering individuals a more profound comprehension of Dharma.

The Significance of Action in Dharma

The concept of karma, which refers to actions, is inherently interconnected with dharma. According to Krishna, fulfilling one's Dharma requires the emphasis and implementation of action. The guidance provided to Arjuna emphasizes the importance of him carrying out his warrior duties, as neglecting them would go against his moral obligations.

One of the key principles emphasized in the Gita is the concept of 'Nishkama Karma', which encourages individuals to engage in actions without becoming attached to the outcomes. Krishna's counsel to Arjuna emphasizes the importance of performing his duty with no attachment to the result, regardless of whether it brings success or failure, victory or defeat. The presence of detachment in this situation guarantees actions are guided by a strong sense of duty, rather than being motivated by the desire for rewards or fear of consequences.

According to Krishna's teachings, he advocates actions should be carried out as a selfless service to others. The transformation brought about by this approach involves changing self-serving activities into offerings that align with the principles of righteousness and Dharma.

The Universal Law of Duty

The teachings of Krishna shed light on the fact that Dharma transcends personal obligations. Every person, by their actions and their dedication to fulfilling their Dharma, plays a crucial role in maintaining the equilibrium of this cosmic balance.

The concept of Dharma not only focuses on individual moral duties, but also places great importance on maintaining societal harmony. When every individual in society fulfills their responsibilities with sincerity and integrity, it significantly contributes to the overall welfare and effective functioning of the community.

The Gita provides a profound understanding of Dharma, and its principles have transcended time, making them timeless. Their guidance is aimed at helping individuals lead a life filled with purpose and righteousness, while effectively managing their personal obligations alongside their duties towards society.

Implementing Dharma in Modern Life

When considering the complexities of modern life, it becomes clear that comprehending one's Dharma causes deep self-reflection regarding their responsibilities within the realms of family, society, and profession. In order to determine if one's actions and decisions align with ethical principles and societal good, it is necessary to conduct an assessment.

The teachings of Krishna offer valuable guidance in helping us maintain a balance between our personal and professional responsibilities. The importance of maintaining this balance cannot be overstated, as it determines a life that is both successful in worldly matters and morally fulfilling.

Today, where material success and personal gain often take precedence, the Gita's emphasis on Dharma acts as a powerful reminder to prioritize decisions that are not only morally upright but also aligned with one's authentic responsibilities.

The process of understanding and incorporating Dharma into our daily lives requires us to develop a strong sense of duty towards ourselves, others, and the greater good. By promoting actions that are beneficial not only for oneself but also for the community and the world, it fosters a sense of responsibility and collective well-being.

To conclude, the teachings of the Bhagavad Gita on Dharma offer profound insights into the principles of leading a life dedicated to duty, righteousness, and ethical action. Achieving personal growth and promoting harmony on both societal and cosmic levels becomes possible when we grasp the essence of our Dharma, faithfully fulfill our obligations, and detach ourselves from the outcomes. The dialogue between Krishna and Arjuna serves as a powerful illustration of the path of Dharma, which continues to shine as a guiding light for navigating life's moral complexities and for making decisions that resonate with our deepest truths and highest principles.

The Path of Righteous Decision-Making

In the Bhagavad Gita, an ancient Hindu scripture, the deep and meaningful conversation between Lord Krishna and Arjuna serves as a valuable source of guidance for those who desire to make righteous decisions. The path that is based on the principles of detachment from outcomes, wisdom, and finding a balance between personal desires and societal expectations, provides timeless insights for individuals who wish to live their lives with integrity and purpose.

Detachment from Outcomes

Among the many crucial teachings that Krishna imparts to Arjuna, one of the most pivotal ones emphasizes the importance of remaining detached from the results that arise from one's actions. Krishna, upon witnessing Arjuna's reluctance to engage in battle, highlights the significance of acting without being emotionally invested in the result, be it victory or defeat.

The principle, which is called Nishkama Karma, refers to the concept of carrying out one's responsibilities without being attached to the results. Krishna clarifies that even though we possess the power to control our actions, the results are not always within our jurisdiction, as they are subject to the influence of multiple external factors beyond our individual control.

When individuals detach themselves from the outcomes, they can maintain moral clarity and direct their focus towards the righteousness of the action itself. The detachment being referred to here is not a manifestation of indifference, but a deep comprehension that genuine satisfaction is derived from wholeheartedly fulfilling one's duties to the best of their capabilities.

Detachment encompasses the act of surpassing the ego and its desires as well. The main point here is to understand that we need to release our attachment to being the sole doers and instead realize that we are just instruments in a much larger cosmic will.

The Role of Wisdom and Discernment

According to Krishna, the act of making righteous decisions causes the possession of both wisdom and discernment. This wisdom goes beyond mere intellect and encompasses a profound comprehension that arises from a blend of personal experiences, introspection, and spiritual enlightenment.

Viveka, or discernment, is the skill of distinguishing between actions that are convenient and those that are morally right, as well as between actions that foster spiritual growth and those that bring about entanglement.

Krishna puts a strong emphasis on the importance of meditation and reflective practices as effective methods for nurturing and developing wisdom. By practicing meditation, individuals can still their minds, achieve mental clarity, and cultivate the inner peace that is essential for making wise decisions.

The teachings of the Gita, along with the wisdom imparted by sages and scriptures, are invaluable resources that can assist in the cultivation of discernment. One can find guidance for their choices and actions through the moral and ethical frameworks they offer.

Balancing Personal Desires and Societal Expectations

One of the key aspects of Krishna's counsel to Arjuna is the exploration of the conflict between personal desires and societal duties. His guidance leads Arjuna to prioritize his Dharma as a warrior over his personal attachments and aversions, even when they are in conflict.

According to the teachings of the Gita, individuals are encouraged to align their actions in a way that balances personal fulfillment and the greater good of society. When deciding, it is important to consider the impact of one's actions on the community and society in order to practice righteous decision-making.

By acting in a way that benefits society, individuals can meet the expectations set by the community. The act of selfless service allows individuals to shift their focus from personal ambition to making valuable contributions to a larger cause.

Implementing Righteous Decision-Making

The essence of this teaching lies in its encouragement for us to base our decision-making in everyday life on ethical principles and the greater good, rather than being driven by personal gain or the fear of negative outcomes.

For the professional sphere, this principle serves as a compass, reminding us to approach our work with unwavering integrity and dedication, while avoiding an excessive attachment to external rewards or recognition.

With personal relationships, this wisdom advises us to approach others with love, compassion, and understanding, while also reminding us not to become too attached to how they respond to or the outcomes of our actions.

In social and community interactions, making righteous decisions revolves around engaging in actions that actively contribute to the promotion of harmony, equity, and the overall well-being of all individuals who are part of the community.

Challenges in Practicing Righteous Decision-Making

Overcoming personal biases and emotional impulses is one challenge individuals face when practicing this path. It is necessary to maintain constant self-awareness and vigilance in order to achieve this.

This approach emphasizes the importance of deep introspection and seeking guidance from wise counsel when confronted with complex situations where the correct course of action is unclear.

Moral courage is often necessary for making righteous decisions, especially when those decisions may face resistance or prove to be difficult to put into action.

In conclusion, it can be stated that the path of righteous decision-making, which is thoroughly explained in the Bhagavad Gita, provides a deep and meaningful framework for effectively navigating the various challenges that life presents. When individuals practice detachment from outcomes, nurture wisdom and discernment, and find a harmonious balance between personal desires and societal responsibilities, they can make choices that are not only ethically sound but also under the profound principles of Dharma. This path has a dual impact: it not only leads to personal growth and fulfillment, but it also contributes to the creation of a just and harmonious society.

Implementing Krishna's Teachings in Modern Life

The Bhagavad Gita, a sacred text originating in ancient India, contains a vast amount of knowledge and teachings that continue to hold great significance in today's modern society. The teachings, conveyed by Lord Krishna to the warrior Arjuna, extend beyond the confines of a historical battle and instead provide timeless wisdom for navigating the challenges of the present-day world. In this exploration, we aim to examine the ways in which we can incorporate these timeless teachings into our everyday existence, placing particular emphasis on the significance of practicing mindfulness, engaging in self-reflection, and aligning our actions with our core values and dharma.

Applying Ancient Wisdom Today

The Bhagavad Gita, while being rooted in an ancient setting, tackles a range of fundamental human concerns, including ethical dilemmas, the quest for purpose, positing inner peace, and the nature of reality. The relevance of these remains constant, both in the present day and as it did thousands of years ago.

In the fast-paced world we live in today, where material pursuits and constant change dominate, the teachings of the Gita serve as a source of stabilizing wisdom. Its emphasis on inner balance, duty, and detachment provides a counterbalance to the often chaotic and superficial aspects of modern life.

The Gita offers valuable insights into ethical living, which are especially relevant in a time where the distinction between right and wrong is often muddled. Its function as a moral compass allows us to make choices that not only serve our own interests but also align with the greater good.

Mindfulness in Everyday Actions

One of the key aspects of Krishna's teachings is the emphasis placed on the significance of living a life filled with awareness and mindfulness. Making a habit of being mindful of everything we do allows us to be conscious of our intentions, live under our values, and enhance our overall sense of wellness.

Engaging in mindful living requires making deliberate choices and consciously deciding how to live. It is crucial to recognize the influence our choices have, not only on ourselves, but also on the environment and the people in our lives.

When individuals are striving to achieve their ambitions and fulfill their responsibilities, practicing mindfulness can play a crucial role in ensuring a harmonious equilibrium between personal desires and obligations. By allowing for a deeper engagement with life, one can break free from the automatic patterns of behavior.

The Importance of Self-Reflection

In order to comprehend and fully grasp one's dharma, which is essentially their righteous duty or life path, it is crucial to engage in self-reflection. By taking the time to reflect on our roles, responsibilities, and actions, we can gain a deeper understanding of our purpose and identify the various ways in which we can fulfill it.

Engaging in regular self-reflection is beneficial, as it assists us in aligning our actions with our core values. One benefit of this is that it encourages introspection, allowing us to delve into our motives, desires, and the potential consequences of our actions.

According to the Gita, meditation is a powerful tool for self-reflection, emphasizing its significance. The process helps us develop a profound sense of self-awareness and clarity, which in turn guides us in making decisions that are in harmony with our true nature and dharma.

Integrating Dharma in Professional Life

Krishna's teachings have a profound impact on us, encouraging us to maintain a high standard of ethical behavior in our professional lives. For fulfilling our obligations, it is essential that we approach them with integrity, honesty, and a strong sense of responsibility towards society.

When we view work as a service, which is known as karma yoga, and as an opportunity to fulfill our dharma, our approach to professional responsibilities undergoes a transformative shift. By encouraging it, a spirit of selflessness and dedication is nurtured.

The teachings of the Gita are beneficial in the professional realm as they help find a balance between ambition and ethics. The guidance it provides helps us in our pursuit of success, all the while ensuring that we remain grounded in moral principles.

Nurturing Relationships through Gita's Wisdom

The principles of empathy, compassion, and understanding, which are emphasized in the teachings of the Gita, play a crucial role in fostering harmonious relationships within personal and social domains.

Practicing detachment, as Krishna advises, does not imply having a lack of interest in relationships. Rather than doing the opposite, it actually fosters emotional intelligence, which is the Skillset of effectively controlling our emotions and comprehending the emotions of others.

In its teachings, the Gita emphasizes the crucial role of selfless love in fostering strong relationships. By fulfilling our duties towards family and friends with selfless love, not only do we enrich our relationships, but we also enhance the quality of our lives.

Facing Life's Challenges with Krishna's Teachings

The teachings found within the Gita offer individuals both strength and a unique perspective when confronted with the various challenges that life presents. One lesson they impart on us is the need to stay unwavering in our principles and responsibilities, even when confronted with challenges.

The advice that Krishna gives to Arjuna regarding finding inner peace amid turmoil is especially relevant. No matter the external circumstances, it serves as a guide for us to find peace and clarity within ourselves.

The teachings of the Gita serve as a constant source of inspiration, motivating us to lead a life filled with purpose and meaning. The encouragement we receive pushes us to discover our true calling and commit ourselves to it wholeheartedly, fueled by passion and unwavering determination.

In conclusion, it can be said that the teachings of the Bhagavad Gita, which were imparted by Krishna himself, provide priceless guidance that can help individuals live a meaningful and morally upright life in today's fast-paced and ever-changing world. Through the application of these teachings in our daily actions, decision-making processes, professional responsibilities, and relationships, we can successfully navigate the intricate web of complexities that characterize contemporary life, fostering greater wisdom, balance, and a sense of purpose. The wisdom found in The Gita, which is timeless, serves as a valuable tool for cultivating a life filled with mindfulness, ethical integrity, and self-reflection, ultimately guiding us towards the discovery of our true dharma and granting us a profound understanding of our role in the world.

Overcoming Inner Conflicts: A Deeper Exploration

Harnessing Inner Strength and Wisdom

Krishna's teachings surpass ordinary advice, delving into deeper philosophical truths. The foundation of this belief is based on the comprehension of one's higher self, which is enduring and timeless, unlike the fleeting challenges of the world.

In the Gita, it is recommended that individuals engage in regular spiritual practices, such as meditation, yoga, and chanting, as these activities serve as effective means to enhance and reinforce the connection with one's inner self. The practices mentioned here are beneficial as they aid in the development of inner calm and clarity, which is crucial for overcoming doubts and fears.

Krishna, in his teachings, presents the path of devotion as an incredibly effective method for cultivating inner strength. Bhakti yoga, also known as the yoga of devotion, is a practice that revolves around surrendering oneself to a higher power and nurturing a profound, intimate connection with the divine. This connection not only grants individuals immense inner strength but also cultivates resilience within them.

Building inner strength can also be achieved by emulating Krishna's attributes, including compassion, wisdom, and equanimity. The cultivation of these qualities offers individuals an effective base of morals and emotions, enabling them to navigate and overcome the adversities of life robustly.

Embracing Life's Challenges as Opportunities for Growth

Krishna, in his wisdom, encourages Arjuna to view adversity not as a setback, but as a powerful force that can ignite personal growth and transformation. The explanation he provides is that when faced with challenges, we are compelled to confront our limitations, fears, and false perceptions, resulting in personal growth and increased self-awareness.

Every single challenge that comes our way presents us with a chance to develop and strengthen our character. It is through facing and overcoming challenging experiences that individuals often develop qualities like courage, perseverance, and integrity.

Krishna places great emphasis on the practice of Karma Yoga, which involves carrying out one's duties without being attached to the results, to turn difficulties into chances for spiritual development. Even when faced with difficult situations, individuals can achieve inner balance and peace by prioritizing their duty rather than focusing on the outcome.

The Gita repeatedly emphasizes the significance of comprehending and following one's Dharma, or moral obligation, when confronted with difficulties. Krishna offers guidance that embracing and fulfilling one's Dharma, even in the face of difficulty, will ultimately result in personal growth and alignment with the cosmic order.

The Role of Discernment in Overcoming Conflicts

In his teachings, Krishna emphasizes the significance of Viveka, which is the ability to differentiate between the eternal and the transient, as well as distinguishing between what is right and what is wrong. The ability to discern is of utmost importance in resolving internal conflicts and making sound judgments.

Krishna's teachings serve as a guiding light, showing us the importance of finding a balance between our emotional instincts and rational thought. Achieving and maintaining a sense of balance is vital for effectively navigating inner conflicts, as it prevents us from being overwhelmed by extreme emotions or rigid reasoning.

Acting as a guru, Krishna takes on the responsibility of providing personalized guidance to Arjuna in the Gita. In today's contemporary society, the act of seeking the counsel and guidance of a knowledgeable mentor or teacher has proven to be of utmost importance, as it can provide immeasurable value to gain clarity and effectively addressing internal conflicts.

Integrating Gita's Teachings in Personal Development

The principal aim of Krishna's teachings is to attain self-realization, which entails recognizing and understanding one's true self. Recognizing this truth is essential for resolving internal conflicts, as it surpasses the dichotomies of pain and pleasure, as well as success and failure.

The teachings of the Gita go beyond spirituality and encompass principles of ethical living and social responsibility as well. When we choose to live our lives in alignment with ethical principles and remain conscious of the effects, our actions have on others, we can effectively navigate the internal conflicts that arise from moral dilemmas and societal pressures.

Krishna's guidance provides valuable counsel for navigating the material world in a mindful and conscientious manner, helping individuals avoid becoming entangled in its intricacies and allurements.

In summary, it can be concluded that the teachings of the Bhagavad Gita provide a comprehensive and invaluable guide for individuals seeking to overcome internal conflicts. Individuals have the potential to achieve a state of inner harmony and continual personal growth by harnessing their inner strength, embracing life's challenges as opportunities for growth, practicing discernment, and pursuing a path of ethical and mindful living. The journey through these teachings is not only transformative, but it also has the power to elevate individuals, guiding them towards a more profound self-awareness and a broader comprehension of the cosmic reality.

Conclusion: Embracing Life's Dharma

Despite being set in an ancient era, the dialogue between Krishna and Arjuna delves into fundamental aspects of human existence, such as duty, morality, purpose, and positing inner peace. The wisdom that encapsulates the principles of Dharma continues to be relevant in our modern times, just as it was during the era of the Mahabharata.

The teachings that are at the core of these beliefs revolve around the fundamental principle of Dharma, which encompasses the notions of leading a righteous life and fulfilling one's duties. According to Krishna, he explains that the Dharma of each person is distinct and influenced by their societal position, personal abilities, and life situation. Understanding and fulfilling this Dharma is essential if one desires to lead a life of purpose and integrity.

By studying and understanding the teachings of the Bhagavad Gita, we gain the knowledge and wisdom necessary to effectively navigate the complexities and overcome the challenges that arise in our modern lives. By providing a framework for deciding grounded in righteousness, they encourage individuals to move beyond personal gains and instead consider the greater good.

The emphasis in Krishna's counsel lies acting with integrity and wisdom, emphasizing the crucial nature of carrying out one's duties sincerely and without being attached to the consequences. Implementing this approach is essential in order to ensure that our actions align with the goals of societal harmony and personal growth.

The principles outlined in the Bhagavad Gita not only advocate for actions that bring benefit to the individual, but also promote the well-being of society. When we fully embrace and incorporate these teachings into our lives, we actively contribute to the development and establishment of a world that is characterized by justice, compassion, and harmony.

Timeless Guidance for Righteous Living

Through its profound teachings, the Bhagavad Gita illuminates the path to righteous living, offering invaluable guidance. The timeless wisdom contained within it serves as a guiding light for individuals who aspire to live a life filled with purpose, integrity, and wisdom, rendering it an invaluable asset for personal and spiritual growth within our modern society.

Chapter Four

Chapter 4: Rukmini's Love

Understanding Devotion and Partnership

The Tale of Krishna and Rukmini

Among the various tales within Hindu mythology, the narrative of Krishna and Rukmini shines brightly as an extraordinary divine union that was predetermined by the cosmos. Rukmini, who is widely regarded as an embodiment of the divine goddess Lakshmi, is fated to unite with Krishna, who is believed to be an incarnation of the mighty deity Vishnu.

Rukmini has always felt a powerful attraction to Krishna, starting from a young age, as she heard stories about his virtues and divine nature. Over time, her devotion towards him continues to grow and strengthens into a profound spiritual love that goes beyond the limitations of the physical realm. The devotion that is displayed in this instance lays a sound foundation for their relationship, effectively establishing a precedent for what is commonly perceived as the perfect and exemplary spiritual union.

During a time when royal marriages were commonly based on convenience and political alliances, Rukmini's unwavering resolve to be with Krishna, motivated by love and a deep spiritual connection, challenges the established social norms and expectations.

Rukmini's Letter to Krishna

When Rukmini finds herself on the brink of being forced into an unwanted marriage with Shishupala, a prince handpicked by her brother, she takes a courageous action, marking a pivotal moment in their story. With the help of a faithful Brahmin, she sends a letter to Krishna to convey her deepest desires.

Rukmini expresses her deep devotion and immense love for Krishna in the letter she wrote. With unwavering conviction, she declares her faith in him and expresses her resolute determination to marry no one but him. This letter is not just a plea for rescue; it is a testament to her clarity, courage, and deep spiritual connection with Krishna.

It was surprising and innovative that Rukmini sent the letter. By breaking conventions, she not only defies societal norms but also emphasizes her agency in making choices that shape her life's path. Through this action, she shows not only her inner strength, but also the profound devotion she has for Krishna.

The Culmination of Divine Love

In response to Rukmini's deep devotion and love, Krishna, who shares the same sentiments, embarks on a journey to Vidarbha, the kingdom ruled by Rukmini. Taking a dramatic course of action, he kidnaps her, following the traditional custom of Kshatriya marriages during that period, thereby thwarting the plans of her brother and Shishupala.

The wedding of Krishna and Rukmini, which took place in the city of Dwarka, is a lavish and extravagant event, filled with immense happiness and excitement. The union between Vishnu and Lakshmi is perceived as a sacred convergence, an eternal bond that was predetermined and sanctioned by the divine laws.

In contrast to many conventional narratives of that era, the bond shared between Krishna and Rukmini is distinguished by a foundation of mutual respect, deep admiration, and a sense of true equality. Despite her deep devotion to Krishna, Rukmini is depicted as a strong and independent person in her own regard.

The tale of Krishna and Rukmini goes beyond its mythological roots and provides timeless teachings on love, devotion, and the importance of spiritual companionship. Their story serves as a source of inspiration and guidance for many individuals who seek to understand the fundamental qualities of a relationship that is rooted in a deep spiritual connection, mutual respect, and divine affection. It is a remarkable testament to the concept that genuine love, when accompanied by unyielding faith and unwavering dedication, possesses the immense strength to triumph over every obstacle that may arise.

Exploring the Themes of Love and Devotion

The story of Krishna and Rukmini, known for its spiritual and emotional depth, provides deep and meaningful insights into the themes of love and devotion, making it an incredibly profound narrative. The relationship between them, which is celebrated in Hindu mythology, serves as an example of unconditional love, devotion as a means to connect with the divine, and the embodiment of mutual respect and equality in a spiritual partnership. The purpose of this exploration is to uncover the profound spiritual dimensions that lie beneath the surface and contribute to the bond between these themes.

Unconditional Love

The love that Rukmini has for Krishna is characterized by its complete and unconditional nature. This love is not bound by the physical realm, as it is deeply rooted in a spiritual connection and a profound admiration that is beyond human understanding. The love she has for Krishna is not driven by any material desires or expectations, but it is a profound reflection of the deep bond her soul shares with the divine.

This type of love surpasses all material conditions and societal norms. This love is beyond the constraints of time and physical boundaries, serving as a testament to the everlasting link between the soul and the divine.

Rukmini's deep affection towards Krishna is a testament to the ability of divine love to manifest and thrive in human connections. Through this illustration, we can clearly see how love, when experienced in its purest form, can transcend the ordinary and bring about a profound spiritual significance to the human existence.

Through the tale of Krishna and Rukmini, we witness the extraordinary strength of unconditional love as it conquers formidable hurdles. Driven by her profound love for Krishna, Rukmini's determination becomes the driving force behind her ability to surpass societal barriers and familial opposition in order to be by his side.

Devotion as a Path to the Divine

One of the key paths to spiritual enlightenment in Hindu philosophy is Bhakti Yoga, which is exemplified by Rukmini's unwavering devotion to Krishna. Her devotion goes beyond being just an emotional expression; it is a spiritual practice that guides her towards the divine.

Rukmini's connection with Krishna is a powerful demonstration of how love can be transformed into a spiritual discipline. Reverence, selflessness, and an intense yearning for spiritual union with the divine are the qualities that define her love.

The transformative nature of Rukmini's devotion knows no bounds, as it touches not only her own life but also profoundly affects the lives of those in her vicinity. The illustration provided truly exemplifies the transformative power of unwavering commitment, leading to a deep spiritual awakening and a level of fulfillment that surpasses conventional experiences of love and affection.

Rukmini's devotion to Krishna transcends mere idolatry or superficial worship, as it contains an element that surpasses conventional practices. This commitment, which touches upon every aspect of her life, serves as a guiding force for her actions, thoughts, and spiritual path.

Mutual Respect and Equality

Although Krishna possesses a divine nature, his relationship with Rukmini is characterized by a strong sense of equality and mutual respect. By challenging the conventional dynamics frequently found in mythological narratives, this aspect establishes a new standard for spiritual partnerships.

Their relationship is rooted in the mutual respect that Krishna and Rukmini have for one another. Despite Krishna's status as a supreme deity, he still values and honors Rukmini's individuality, choices, and devotion, while Rukmini, on her part, deeply respects Krishna's divine mission and wisdom.

The relationship they share serves as a perfect example of how spiritual partnerships thrive when there is mutual support and understanding. Their relationship is characterized by the way they enhance each other's strengths and provide unwavering support in their spiritual and worldly endeavors.

The relationship between Krishna and Rukmini serves as a perfect example of how two partners in a spiritual relationship can experience personal growth and learning together. The interactions between them, as well as the experiences they share, provide valuable opportunities for both parties to grow and grow spiritually.

To summarize, the story of Krishna and Rukmini delves into the themes of love and devotion, providing profound understandings about the essence of spiritual connections. The union between them serves as a prime example of how unconditional love and devotion can lead to spiritual enlightenment, as well as highlighting the significance of mutual respect and equality within partnerships. The story goes beyond the limits of time and culture, offering eternal wisdom on how relationships can serve as a potent catalyst for spiritual development and personal satisfaction.

Spiritual Partnership: The Union of Krishna and Rukmini

The relationship between Krishna and Rukmini, as portrayed in Hindu mythology, serves as a profound illustration of how connections can transcend mere physical and emotional realms, transforming into a shared voyage of spiritual development and advancement. The union between them is marked by qualities that complement each other, shared spiritual goals, and a strong foundation of trust and faith, which offers profound insights into what a spiritual partnership truly embodies.

Complementing Each Other

The partnership between Krishna and Rukmini is marked by a perfect equilibrium of qualities. Krishna's divine attributes and wisdom are beautifully complemented by Rukmini's unwavering devotion and inner strength. The combination of these qualities serves as a prime example of how partners in a spiritual relationship can effectively amplify and harmonize each other's individual strengths and weaknesses.

The demonstration of their relationship highlights the potential for spiritual partnerships to facilitate individual development. The spiritual and personal development of each partner is enhanced by the contributions of the other, thanks to their unique attributes and insights. Krishna and Rukmini consistently uncover novel perspectives and enhance their understanding of one another through their interactions, leading to mutual growth.

As they embark on their journey together, Krishna and Rukmini establish a strong bond of support, nurturing each other's spiritual quests and endeavors. It is important to note that this support is not passive; rather, it requires active participation and encouragement in one another's spiritual goals and aspirations.

Shared Spiritual Goals

The bond shared by Krishna, and Rukmini surpasses the typical understanding of marital alliances. The foundation of their union lies in their shared spiritual goals and values, which transforms their relationship into a journey of mutual spiritual advancement instead of a mere worldly association.

Their union is marked by a firm determination to uphold dharma (righteousness) and a collective pursuit of spiritual truths. The common aim they share directs their relationship towards higher purposes and the attainment of spiritual fulfillment as a group.

Krishna and Rukmini, as a united pair, actively take part in various spiritual practices that deepen their understanding and strengthen their bond with the divine. The partnership between them transforms into a sacred space where they can explore and seek enlightenment on a spiritual level, as they both provide support and encouragement to one another in their individual spiritual practices.

Learning and growing together is a fundamental element of our spiritual partnership. By engaging in shared experiences, facing challenges together, and practicing spiritual disciplines, Krishna and Rukmini constantly grow and deepen their comprehension and encounter with the divine.

The Role of Trust and Faith

The foundation of Krishna and Rukmini's relationship is built on trust, which is the bedrock of their bond. Even when confronted with difficulties, Rukmini's unwavering trust in Krishna's divine nature and wisdom persists. Rukmini's devotion and strength are deeply trusted by Krishna, creating a reciprocal trust between them.

The story revolves around Rukmini's powerful belief in the sanctity of their union, which is a central theme. Reflecting her deep spiritual understanding and unwavering commitment, her belief in the divine will and the destined nature of their relationship remains steadfast.

The journey of Krishna and Rukmini is filled with many trials and tribulations, which they conquer by relying on their deep-rooted faith in each other and in the greater divine blueprint. Their strong faith enables them to face and overcome difficulties with grace and fortitude.

The foundation of trust within their partnership acts as a catalyst, igniting and fueling their spiritual growth. With this secure foundation, both individuals can fearlessly and confidently explore their spiritual paths, knowing that they can rely on each other's unwavering support.

The Dynamics of a Spiritual Partnership

Despite being divine, Krishna and their relationship with others is characterized by a sense of equality. Rukmini is held in high regard and treated as an equal partner, with her opinions and contributions being highly respected. Any spiritual partnership relies heavily on the existence of mutual respect.

The interactions between Krishna and Rukmini illustrate effective communication and a deep level of understanding. They actively listen, promptly respond, and actively engage with one another in a manner that reveals a profound sense of empathy and a comprehensive understanding of each other's unique perspectives.

Krishna and Rukmini, being partners, jointly shoulder the responsibilities and duties that come with their worldly roles and their spiritual endeavors. Through the sharing of responsibilities, they show the collaborative essence of their partnership.

The key to a successful spiritual partnership lies in the mutual nurturing of each other's spiritual aspirations. Through their mutual encouragement and unwavering support for each other's spiritual ambitions, Krishna and Rukmini show this principle.

To conclude, it is important to recognize that the spiritual partnership between Krishna and Rukmini is a remarkable example that highlights how relationships can play a significant role in facilitating spiritual development and personal transformation. By combining complementing qualities, shared spiritual goals, and a foundation of trust and faith, their union offers valuable lessons on the dynamics of a spiritual partnership. This highlights the significance of these relationships in terms of their potential to promote personal growth, deepen one's spiritual understanding, and establish a supportive atmosphere for mutual spiritual advancement.

Lessons from Rukmini and Krishna's Relationship

The deep bond between Lord Krishna and Rukmini, characterized by their unwavering devotion and profound respect for each other, offers valuable insights into the intricate dynamics of spiritual partnership. By going beyond the typical love stories, their narrative highlights the true nature of love, personal development, and the importance of supporting one another. In this thorough and comprehensive exploration, we delve deep into the many different aspects and facets of their relationship, revealing valuable lessons that remain just as pertinent in today's world as they were during the mythical era of their divine union.

Understanding True Love

The love that Krishna and Rukmini share surpasses the limitations of the physical and mundane aspects of life. The love being referred to is one that is firmly grounded in spirituality and devotion, underscoring the transcendent aspect of genuine love.

According to the principles of Hindu philosophy, the affectionate bond existing between Krishna and Rukmini is frequently interpreted as a mirror image of the profound adoration that the soul possesses for the divine. This example beautifully showcases how human relationships can reflect the soul's deep longing for a profound connection with the spiritual realm.

The defining characteristics of their love are its selflessness and unconditional nature. No matter the circumstances, Rukmini's love for Krishna remains unrestricted by worldly conditions.

Complementing Each Other

The relationship between Krishna and Rukmini serves as a perfect example of how partners can effectively complement each other's strengths and weaknesses. The harmonious union between Krishna and Rukmini is achieved through a perfect balance of Rukmini's unwavering devotion and strength, which complements Krishna's divine qualities.

Through their partnership, they create an environment that nurtures personal growth and encourages spiritual evolution. Their mutual support for each other aids in their spiritual growth, enabling them to reach their fullest potential.

Both Krishna and Rukmini, within the bounds of this spiritual partnership, contribute to the enhancement and elevation of each other's inherent attributes. Rukmini's unwavering devotion has the remarkable ability to reveal Krishna's compassionate and loving nature, while Krishna's divine essence simultaneously deepens Rukmini's spiritual comprehension.

Shared Spiritual Goals

Krishna and Rukmini's connection goes beyond being a simple marital alliance. The shared spiritual goals and values that they both have serve as the foundation of their relationship.

Joined, they venture forth on a path of spiritual development, side by side. Through their relationship, they embark on a path that leads them to a deeper understanding of spirituality and a higher state of enlightenment.

The example of Krishna and Rukmini perfectly illustrates how a couple's spiritual aspirations can align and merge, resulting in a relationship that is not only fulfilling but also deeply profound.

The Role of Trust and Faith

Trust is the fundamental element that strengthens the bond between Krishna and Rukmini, forming the bedrock of their relationship. Central to the narrative of Rukmini and Krishna is Rukmini's unwavering belief in Krishna's wisdom and divine nature.

Rukmini's unwavering faith in Krishna's divine will and the sanctity of their union serves as a powerful testament to the profound depth of her devotion. Instead of being blind faith, her belief is founded on a profound spiritual understanding and a strong bond with Krishna.

By sharing their story, they show the essential nature of trust and faith for overcoming the challenges that life presents. Strengthened by their unshakeable belief in each other and in the greater purpose, they courageously navigate through a series of trials and tribulations.

Partnership in Life's Journey

With Krishna and Rukmini, their relationship stands as a shining example of a genuine partnership, where both individuals wholeheartedly support and uplift one another in every aspect of their lives, including their spiritual journeys.

The basis of their relationship is characterized by a strong sense of interdependence and cooperation. With mutual respect for each other's roles and contributions, they effectively collaborate and work together, not only in their worldly responsibilities, but also in their spiritual endeavors.

Devotion in Relationships

Love, within the confines of their relationship, transcends and grows into a deep sense of devotion. Rukmini's love for Krishna is characterized by a strong sense of veneration and a profound yearning for spiritual unity.

One cannot help but notice how their relationship beautifully showcases the transformative power of love within a partnership, elevating it to a spiritual level. Through its ability to facilitate the expression and experience of devotion, it effectively enhances and deepens the emotional and spiritual aspects of the relationship.

Balancing Worldly and Spiritual Duties

Krishna and Rukmini, despite being fully engaged in fulfilling their duties in the material world, maintain a deep and unwavering spiritual bond. One important lesson in maintaining harmony in relationships recognizes and maintaining this balance.

The way they live their lives together serves as a powerful example of how spiritual principles can be seamlessly incorporated into one's daily life and obligations. The evidence they provide shows that spirituality and worldly obligations can coexist without conflict and can be effectively managed harmoniously.

In sum up, the relationship between Krishna and Rukmini presents deep insights into spiritual partnership. Through their narrative, we learn about essential life lessons, including true love, the power of mutual support, positing shared spiritual aspirations, the value of trust and faith, and the art of maintaining an equilibrium between worldly responsibilities and spiritual growth. This serves as an inspiring example, showcasing how relationships have the potential to go beyond physical and worldly boundaries, growing into a shared spiritual journey that brings fulfillment and mutual growth. That their union is divine serves as a remarkable testament to the extraordinary power of spiritual love and the limitless potential of relationships to facilitate profound spiritual growth.

Conclusion: Embracing Love and Devotion

The Essence of Divine Love

The story of Krishna and Rukmini takes the idea of love beyond just a simple emotional or physical connection and transforms it into a profound, spiritual journey. Their love, which is infused with unwavering dedication and a deep sense of mutual admiration, surpasses the traditional limitations of romantic love, providing a glimpse into the ethereal realm of divine love.

The bond between Krishna and Rukmini is marked by an unconditional and selfless love that knows no bounds. This pure expression of the soul's longing for union with the divine is not restricted by any worldly conditions or expectations.

Story they tell serves as a symbol, illustrating how human relationships can mirror the profound longing of the soul for a deeper connection with the divine. How this exemplifies love, at its utmost level, to spiritual awakening and fulfillment, is quite remarkable.

Devotion as a Pathway to Spiritual Growth

Bhakti (devotion) is the very core of their relationship, flowing through every aspect. That Rukmini is so devoted to Krishna not only reflects her love for him, but also serves as evidence of her spiritual growth and deep comprehension.

Their relationship encompasses not only a journey of the heart, but also a profound journey of the soul. The journey I am referring to encapsulates the various trials, tribulations, joys, and the ultimate bliss that come with spiritual progression.

Rukmini's dedication to her faith extends beyond the customary bounds of worship. The holistic nature of Bhakti is beautifully reflected in her life and being, making it a breathing experience that encompasses every aspect.

Mutual Respect and Equality in Partnership

Even though Krishna is divine, his relationship with Rukmini is marked by equality. This serves as a powerful testament to the importance of mutual respect and understanding in spiritual partnerships.

The bond between them serves as a prime example of genuine spiritual companionship. Through their shared commitment to spiritual growth, they offer mutual support, walking hand in hand, leveraging each other's strengths, and embarking on a transformative journey together.

The foundation of their relationship is built upon respect. The bond between individuals is nurtured and strengthened when there is respect for each other's individuality, choices, and spiritual paths.

Lessons for Contemporary Relationships

One of the key lessons we can learn from the story of Krishna and Rukmini is the importance of integrating spirituality into our relationships. This perspective encourages us to see our partnerships as more than just emotional bonds; they are spiritual journeys that have the potential to bring us greater self-awareness and fulfillment.

By sharing their story, they offer a valuable guide for those seeking to establish relationships that prioritize devotion, respect, and mutual growth. When relationships are grounded in these values, it becomes clear how they can flourish and result in deep personal growth and spiritual advancement.

The demonstration of their union highlights the successful balancing act between spiritual obligations and worldly commitments. The illustration highlights the notion that one's spiritual journey and daily life can intertwine and complement each other.

Embracing the Divine in Relationships

Through the story of Krishna and Rukmini, we are encouraged to acknowledge and appreciate the divine essence that exists within our partners. It serves as a reminder to explore beyond the surface level of existence, delving into the spiritual realm that connects us all.

Their love story beckons us to explore love on a profound level, transcending the ordinary and delving into a realm where love serves as a bridge to our higher selves and divine connection.

To conclude, "Rukmini's Love: Understanding Devotion and Partnership" not only shares the captivating love story of Krishna and Rukmini, but also offers a profound examination of the profound dimensions of love, devotion, and spiritual partnership. Their narrative, exemplifying the profound love and spiritual connection between two individuals, imparts timeless wisdom regarding the ability of relationships to surpass physical and emotional confines, growing into a mutual expedition towards spiritual progress and ultimate contentment. This serves as a powerful example of how love and devotion can elevate human experiences to a divine level, providing valuable insights into how we can incorporate these sacred elements into our own lives and relationships.

Chapter Five

Chapter 5: Sudama's Friendship

The Riches of Humility and Generosity

A Tale of Timeless Friendship

The story of Krishna and Sudama's friendship has been handed down from generation to generation, not only cherished for its mythological importance but also admired for the valuable lessons it teaches about the essence of genuine friendship. The story they share serves as a powerful reminder that genuine friendships are not based on money or social status, but on mutual respect, love, and understanding.

The tale presented here serves as a powerful and eloquent exposition, illustrating the profound message that genuine friendship can surpass and transcend the societal boundaries that are imposed upon us. It illustrates that the purity of friendship lies in its ability to rise above worldly considerations and exist in a realm where the soul's connections are the only currency of value.

The Contrasting Lives of Krishna and Sudama

As an avatar of the god Vishnu, Krishna is held in high regard, not just as a deity, but also as a wise and compassionate king. His life, characterized by opulence, divine miracles, and profound teachings, establishes him as a central figure in Hindu mythology.

Sudama, a humble Brahmin, stands in stark contrast to Krishna's divine stature and regal magnificence, as Sudama's life is marred by poverty. Sudama's circumstances may be impoverished, but his character is defined by the abundance of spirituality, wisdom, and contentment he possesses.

The story of Krishna and Sudama is a fascinating tale that beautifully intertwines two contrasting realms–the realm of the divine and the realm of the mortal, the world of opulence and the world of austerity. However, it is precisely at this point of intersection that their friendship flourishes, unaffected by the differences in their respective worldly circumstances.

The Formation of a Sacred Bond

Their friendship has deep roots that can be traced back to their childhood, when Krishna and Sudama were classmates studying under the same guru. The early years of development serve as the building blocks for a relationship that is marked by innocence, happiness, and a profound spiritual bond.

Within the ashram of their guru, Krishna and Sudama gain a deeper understanding that transcends traditional academic knowledge. The values of empathy, respect, and the essence of Dharma (which refers to righteous living) are imbibed by them, and these values play a vital role in shaping not only their characters but also their friendship.

As time continues to move forward, Krishna and Sudama find their paths separate, ultimately leading them towards distinct and contrasting life journeys. Despite passaging time and the change in circumstances, the bond they share remains strong, which is a testament to the enduring nature of genuine friendship.

The Reunion: A Meeting of Souls

After years of being apart, the eventual reunion of Krishna and Sudama is a poignant and heartwarming moment that adds depth to the story. Unlike typical reunions, this gathering is defined by an overwhelming display of sincere love, respect, and happiness.

Despite the changes in their individual worldly statuses, their meeting remains genuine and free from any superficiality or pretense. The narrative of Krishna, the king, and Sudama, the impoverished Brahmin, is a powerful testament to the unbreakable bond of genuine friendship, as it shows how it remains unchanged despite any external shifts or alterations.

Unveiling the Layers of Their Friendship

Mutual respect and admiration serve as the strong pillars of the relationship between Krishna and Sudama. Krishna, despite being revered as divine, demonstrates a remarkable level of respect and love towards Sudama, valuing and honoring his friend's simplicity and virtue.

Sudama approaches Krishna with pure intentions, completely free from any hidden agendas or desires for material benefits. The pure intention behind his visit to Krishna is solely to reunite with his old friend, a testament to his genuine and unwavering loyalty.

In summary, the narrative of Krishna and Sudama encompasses various stages of their relationship, starting from their innocent companionship in their youth and progressing to a poignant reunion later in life, thereby presenting a remarkable example of a friendship that challenges societal norms and materialistic ideals. The tale they have is not simply a story that can be found only within the confines of mythology. The story captivates the reader by beautifully showcasing and commemorating the profound significance of humility, the noble virtue of generosity, and the unshakeable genuine friendship.

The Value of True Friendship

In the realm of Hindu mythology, the tale of Krishna and Sudama, with its rich historical significance, transcends mere storytelling and delves into the intricate dynamics of divine and human connection. This piece of writing takes a deep dive into the significance of genuine friendship, going beyond superficial factors like money, social status, and the inevitable passage of time. The story presented here unravels a beautiful tapestry of lessons, shining a light on the essence of genuine friendship and highlighting the significance of love, respect, and mutual understanding. In this comprehensive exploration, we will delve into the intricate dynamics of their bond, meticulously unraveling the qualities that set their friendship apart as a shining example of genuine human connection.

Friendship Beyond Materialistic Measures

The story of Krishna and Sudama beautifully captures the true essence of friendship with poignant clarity. The bond that they share goes beyond material gains or social prestige; it is based on a deeper connection that surpasses these worldly measures.

Their friendship is based on a firm foundation of mutual love and respect. Even though there are vast discrepancies between their social and economic standings, their unwavering respect for each other endures. Despite Krishna's regal status as a king and deity, he interacts with Sudama, a humble Brahmin, on fair competition, treating him with genuine affection and equality.

The friendship between them holds great significance because of its remarkable ability to surpass the strict societal norms that were prevalent during their era. This is a relationship that defies the limitations imposed by caste, wealth, and power, proving that genuine friendship knows no bounds and is independent of societal hierarchies.

The primary focus of the story is to draw attention to the stark dichotomy between material wealth and the depth of one's spiritual life. Sudama, despite his poverty in terms of material possessions, possesses a wealth of spirituality and virtue, which deeply resonates with Krishna and forms the core of their extraordinary friendship.

Unwavering Bond Since Childhood

The bond between Krishna and Sudama, which originated in their childhood, is a testament to the purity and unguardedness of their emotions during that time. The bond that they developed in the ashram, which is a hermitage where their guru lives, is marked by genuine affection and camaraderie.

Through the years and the ever-changing circumstances of their lives, their friendship remains strong and unwavering. Even though they have been separated for many years and their individual circumstances have changed dramatically, the bond they share remains untouched and just as strong as it has always been.

The bond between them is sustained by the crucial role that shared experiences and memories from their childhood days play. The memories serve as a bridge, connecting their experiences with the present and emphasizing the profound bond of their friendship.

The story of Krishna and Sudama is a perfect example that showcases the enduring nature of genuine friendships. This shows that relationships that are built on profound human values can endure and overcome the obstacles and transformations that life presents.

Lessons in Empathy and Equality

The display of empathy between Krishna and Sudama plays a crucial role in shaping their relationship. The mutual understanding between Krishna and Sudama is exemplified by Krishna's empathetic understanding of Sudama's humble state and Sudama's empathy towards Krishna's royal duties and responsibilities, showcasing the depth of their connection.

The way they interact with one another directly opposes the hierarchical social structures that were in place during that time period. The act of Krishna welcoming Sudama with open arms, taking the time to wash his feet, and treating him with the utmost respect and honor, is a remarkable demonstration of the value of equality in friendship.

The key message conveyed in the story is the cruciality of valuing and recognizing someone's inner worth instead of placing importance on their external situation. Krishna highly appreciates Sudama and the inner virtues that define him - honesty, devotion, and purity of heart.

The Spiritual Dimension of their Friendship

The friendship that exists between Krishna and Sudama surpasses the boundaries of the material world and explores the depths of the spiritual realm. It is not material gifts or favors that nurture this bond, but the spiritual affinity and mutual respect we share.

Through its narrative, the story embodies the idea of a transcendent and spiritual connection that can be present in human relationships.

In the friendship between Krishna and Sudama, Krishna, being a divine being, acknowledges and honors Sudama's spiritual purity and devotion, thereby elevating their bond to a spiritual plane.

Their friendship serves as a powerful lens through which the narrative imparts significant spiritual insights. One of the important lessons it imparts is the importance of humility, selflessness, and giving with no expectations.

Ultimately, the story of Krishna and Sudama reveals significant revelations about the core essence of friendship. Their relationship acts as a shining beacon, bringing to light the significance of empathy, respect, equality, and spiritual connection in fostering strong friendships. The lesson it imparts is that genuine friendships cannot be defined by superficial measures, but they are cultivated through common values, mutual respect, and an understanding that surpasses worldly standards. The story they shared continues to serve as a timeless reminder, reminding us of the importance of genuine relationships in our lives. It encourages us to actively seek connections that are based on profound human values and treasure them.

Humility and Generosity in the Story of Krishna and Sudama

The story of Krishna and Sudama goes beyond being a simple account of friendship; it serves as a valuable lesson on the virtues of humility and generosity. Both characters exemplify these virtues in their own unique ways, and it is through these virtues that the crux of this timeless tale unfolds, providing deep insights into the nature of human virtue and divine grace. Through this in-depth exploration, we thoroughly examine the intricacies of Sudama's humility and Krishna's generosity, uncovering the multiple layers of these virtues and their profound implications within the story and beyond.

Sudama's Humility

The life of Sudama is a perfect example that portrays humility. Despite facing financial hardships, he finds solace and satisfaction in leading a simple and content life. Even though he faces financial struggles, his humble disposition remains unaffected.

One of the standout qualities of Sudama's character is his incredible lack of envy or resentment towards those who have more than him. What stands out the most is his remarkable humility and acceptance of life's challenges, which is even more remarkable given the dire poverty he faces.

Sudama's visit to Krishna is driven by his genuine and selfless motivations, completely devoid of any materialistic aspirations. The driving force behind his journey to see Krishna is the strong yearning to be reunited with his dear friend, rather than any expectations of receiving financial aid.

The way Sudama lives his life and how he interacts with Krishna exemplifies genuine humility, which is a quality that acknowledges one's position and embraces it with no sense of inferiority or self-pity.

Krishna's Generosity

The way Krishna responded to Sudama's visit is a perfect example of generosity. The understanding he has is that Sudama's veritable treasure lies not in material riches, but in being acknowledged, loved, and respected. Krishna's generosity extends beyond material help and encompasses emotional and spiritual aspects as well.

Through Krishna's actions, it becomes clear that the ultimate satisfaction in giving arises from comprehending and meeting the needs of others, thus experiencing genuine joy. His kindness towards Sudama is a selfless act of love, with no ulterior motives or strings attached.

Krishna, being an incarnation of divinity, displays a level of generosity that goes beyond what is normal for humans. The manner in which he treated Sudama, a poor Brahmin, with the highest level of honor and affection, serves as a shining example of how generosity should be practiced.

The act of Krishna's generosity towards Sudama has the power to bring about transformation. The act of giving not only helps to ease Sudama's material poverty, but it also serves to reaffirm the value of their friendship and the virtues of humility and gratitude.

The Interplay of Humility and Generosity

The interaction that takes place between Krishna and Sudama is a truly beautiful and remarkable display of both humility and generosity. The humility displayed by Sudama triggers Krishna's immense generosity, which then reinforces Sudama's humility and gratitude even more.

Their story is a testament to the importance of moral virtues and serves as a powerful lesson. One of the main teachings is that genuine humility and generosity are not only virtues that deserve admiration, but they are also indispensable qualities for nurturing human connections and cultivating a society built on compassion.

The story goes beyond the boundaries of societal hierarchies and differences in material wealth. The significance of social status and wealth becomes insignificant when considering true virtue.

The Spiritual Significance of Humility and Generosity

It is important to recognize that the virtues of humility and generosity are not just moral attributes, but also serve as pathways to spiritual growth. Sudama's humility and Krishna's generosity are prime examples of how their spiritual development has enriched their characters and outlook on life.

Through its narrative, the story effectively showcases how the embodiment of divine qualities, such as generosity and humility, can transform mundane human interactions into meaningful and spiritually significant moments.

To sum up, the story of Krishna and Sudama serves as a powerful reminder of the enduring significance of humility and generosity, imparting invaluable lessons that remain relevant across generations. Sudama's incredible humility, coupled with Krishna's boundless generosity, serve as a powerful beacon of light, illuminating the transformative potential of these virtues in both individual lives and interpersonal connections. Their story beautifully illustrates how humility and generosity can enhance the human experience, surpassing materialistic endeavors and uplifting the soul. The act of embodying these virtues in our lives not only encourages us, but also contributes to the creation of a world where compassion, understanding, and selfless giving become the cornerstone of human interaction and spiritual fulfillment.

The Spiritual Dimensions of Krishna and Sudama's Friendship

The bond shared between Krishna and Sudama goes beyond the usual connections, creating a beautiful tapestry filled with spiritual symbolism and profound moral teachings. Not only is their story a narrative of earthly interactions, but it also serves as a profound saga that captures the very essence of divine connection and spiritual truths. In this deep and thorough analysis, we embark on a comprehensive exploration of the spiritual aspects of their friendship.

Throughout this journey, we uncover the intricate layers of symbolism, selflessness, and compassion that contribute to making their relationship a true exemplar of divine interaction and human virtue.

A Divine Encounter

The reunion of Krishna and Sudama goes beyond a casual meeting; it symbolizes the rekindling of a deep bond between two dear friends.

The meeting between them serves as a demonstration of how spiritual connections can manifest in human relationships. The key point that is being highlighted is that when these connections are founded on authentic love and spiritual kinship, they elevate human interactions to a realm of divine significance.

By warmly receiving Sudama and acknowledging the purity of his soul, Krishna exemplifies the profound spiritual truth that the value of a person's soul goes beyond their financial or societal circumstances.

Through his simplicity, Sudama serves as a representation of how divinity can appear modestly. Through the character, the lesson is imparted that true spiritual wealth can be found in humility and simplicity, rather than in material possessions.

Lessons in Selflessness and Compassion

The way Krishna treated Sudama serves as a strong and impactful illustration of genuine compassion. Disregarding the societal norms and expectations of a king, he embraces Sudama with utmost love and respect, demonstrating his genuine affection for his friend. By demonstrating such deep-seated compassion and acknowledging Sudama's inner worth, Krishna's actions stand as a testament to his character.

The interaction between Krishna and Sudama transcends the social hierarchies that were prevalent in their era. Krishna, who is not only a revered deity but also a king, impressively exhibits no sense of superiority. Rather than exhibiting arrogance or indifference, his actions show a profound understanding and humility, perfectly encapsulating the essence of divine compassion.

The friendship that they share is a great example, and it teaches the important virtue of selflessness. Krishna's act of generosity towards Sudama is completely selfless and with no hidden agenda. The act in question is one of pure selflessness, with the sole intention of bringing joy and comfort to his friend.

Another key point highlighted in the story is the crucial role of empathetic understanding within relationships. Krishna, with complete understanding of Sudama's pride and reluctance to request aid, ensures that his needs are met while still honoring his self-respect. In any relationship, the significance of sensitivity cannot be overstated, as it serves as a fundamental element in cultivating compassion and understanding.

The Spiritual Essence of Their Bond

The friendship of Krishna and Sudama is characterized by a spiritual essence that is clearly showed because their bond remains unaffected by any material gifts they may exchange. The exchange that truly matters between them is the gift of unconditional love, respect, and spiritual companionship.

The bond that they share can be perceived as a reflection of the profound and unconditional love that is often associated with the divine. This illustrates how genuine friendship mirrors the profound love that is shared between the soul and the divine.

The story of spiritual aspirants serves as a guiding light, shining a bright light on the journey towards divine love, which can be achieved through acts of selflessness, humility, and compassion. The teaching highlights the notion that spiritual development encompasses not only personal enlightenment, but also the upliftment of others.

In summary, the friendship between Krishna and Sudama serves as a powerful story that surpasses conventional ideas about human relationships, shedding light on the spiritual aspects of friendship. Their story beautifully exemplifies how relationships, when characterized by selflessness, compassion, and spiritual connection, can divine interaction and ethical advancement. One of the valuable lessons it imparts is the ability to recognize and appreciate the spiritual essence present in our relationships, motivating us to foster connections that bring emotional and spiritual fulfillment. The enduring friendship they shared continues to serve as a profound testament to the inherent capacity for divine greatness that exists within human bonds, encouraging us to cultivate our own relationships with a similar sense of spirituality, humility, and love.

The Impact of their Friendship

The depiction of the friendship between Krishna and Sudama in Hindu mythology goes well beyond a mere portrayal of a basic connection between two individuals. This transformative journey that it encapsulates serves as a paradigm and sets a new standard for human relationships. Not only does this profound narrative leave a lasting impact on the lives of the characters, but it also serves as a source of timeless lessons on the values of friendship, humility, and generosity. Through this comprehensive exploration, we delve into the profound transformative effects of Sudama and their friendship, and how their story serves as a paradigm for fostering relationships grounded in fundamental human values.

Transformative Effects on Sudama

The visit of Sudama to Krishna serves as a pivotal moment in his life. When he first reaches Krishna's palace, he is a humble and impoverished Brahmin, but when he leaves, there is a miraculous transformation that occurs, not only in terms of his material possessions but more importantly, in his spiritual and emotional well-being.

Despite the significant change in Sudama's material circumstances that occur after his visit, the story's underlying message centers on the reiteration of the significance of friendship. The gesture of Krishna's generosity and kindness towards Sudama surpasses any material possessions, emphasizing the profound emotional and spiritual backing that genuine friends extend to each other.

Sudama's transformation serves as a powerful testament to the importance of possessing virtues such as humility and generosity. The significance of these virtues, humility and generosity, in enhancing the human experience, is highlighted through the example of approaching Krishna with humility and receiving a generous response from him.

Of all the aspects of Sudama's transformation, the spiritual dimension holds the utmost importance. Through his encounter with Krishna, his faith and devotion are reinforced, resulting in a deeper understanding and connection to spirituality.

A Paradigm for Human Relationships

By recounting the tale of Krishna and Sudama, the conventional notion of riches in life is completely transformed. The statement implies that the genuine riches of an individual do not live in their material belongings, but in the values they uphold and the sincerity of their connections.

The friendship between them serves as a perfect example of unwavering support and love that knows no bounds. This lesson emphasizes genuine friends are those who remain loyal and supportive to one another, regardless of their social and economic backgrounds, and offer help with no ulterior motives.

With the narrative, virtues such as kindness, generosity, humility, and selflessness are given higher priority and are considered more valuable than material wealth. By promoting the idea of nurturing these values in relationships, it is believed that individuals can experience a life that is more fulfilling and meaningful.

For social values, the story of Krishna and Sudama has a significant impact. The encouragement of such values fosters a society in which relationships are founded on the principles of mutual respect, understanding, and support, rather than being solely transactional or materialistic.

Lessons for Contemporary Times

The friendship between Krishna and Sudama teaches us valuable lessons that are relevant even today. In today's society, where relationships are often superficial and driven by materialistic values, this story serves as a poignant reminder of the timeless significance of authentic human connections.

The narrative promotes the idea of fostering stronger relationships by emphasizing the importance of mutual respect, empathy, and understanding. The message within this statement prompts us to see past the superficial aspects of wealth and status, and instead, recognize the inherent worth of individuals.

Besides being a captivating narrative, the story also serves as a source of motivation for personal growth and the exploration of one's spiritual journey. By showcasing the impact of friendships, it shows how they can inspire personal growth, spiritual development, and the practice of virtues like humility and generosity.

In summary, the relationship between Krishna and Sudama serves as a powerful narrative, illustrating the significant influence that authentic friendship can bring about. Their narrative is a shining example of how human connections should be, underlining the importance of embracing values like humility, generosity, and unwavering support. This serves as a reminder that the most valuable treasures in life can be found within the meaningful connections we cultivate and the virtues we choose to embrace. This timeless story continues to provide inspiration and direction, reminding us of the importance of embracing the genuine meaning of friendship and nurturing connections that are built on fundamental human values and spiritual ties.

Sudama's Offering: A Symbol of Pure Love

In the poignant tale of Krishna and Sudama, a seemingly insignificant act of kindness takes on profound symbolic meaning as Sudama humbly offers Krishna a handful of rice. Through this gesture and the way Krishna receives the offering, we can clearly see the embodiment of pure love, friendship, and spiritual abundance, surpassing any material wealth. Through a comprehensive analysis, we embark on a detailed exploration where we delve deep into the intricate symbolism of Sudama's offering and Krishna's response, meticulously unraveling the multiple layers of meaning that contribute to making this moment an absolutely pivotal point in the story.

The Handful of Rice

The offering that Sudama presented to Krishna, which was just a small amount of rice, serves as a significant representation of both simplicity and sincerity. The gift that Sudama carried with him when he visited Krishna may be modest, but it is filled with heartfelt sentiment and lacks any opulence or grandeur.

The offering perfectly symbolizes the essence of pure love and friendship. This serves as evidence that genuine connections are not established based on the value of material possessions, but on the genuine intentions and pure sincerity.

In a world where materialism and extravagant demonstrations of love often take center stage, Sudama's act of offering rice serves as a poignant reminder of the importance of simplicity and the true meaning of generosity.

Sudama's offering not only showcases his deep devotion to Krishna, but also highlights his humility. Sudama, despite his impoverished state, brings a humble gift, which reflects his belief that true offerings are measured by sincerity rather than material wealth.

Krishna's Reception of the Gift

The reception that Krishna gives to the humble offering is characterized by a sense of profound gratitude and great reverence. With the utmost respect, he accepts the rice, cherishing it as if it were the most valuable present imaginable.

The response that Krishna gives to Sudama's offering serves as a representation of how the divine acknowledges and appreciates genuine love and affection. The point being made is that with spiritual connections, the intention and love behind a gift hold much more significance than its monetary worth.

The act of Krishna receiving the rice from Sudama is a divine reciprocation of Sudama's love. The belief is that even the smallest offerings, made with genuine intentions, hold as much value as the most extravagant treasures in the eyes of the divine.

In this moment, Krishna's actions go beyond the limitations of materialistic judgments and societal norms. He exemplifies the idea that genuine friendship and love are not dependent on riches or material goods, but on profound emotional and spiritual connections.

Symbolism in Hindu Philosophy

Within the wider framework of Hindu philosophy, specifically in the Bhakti's realm tradition, the act of offering holds immense spiritual meaning, irrespective of the material worth it may possess. The belief is that what truly matters is the devotion and purity of the heart possessed by the individual making the offering.

The acceptance of Sudama's rice by Krishna serves as a valuable lesson in spiritual equality. This statement shows that, according to the divine perspective, all devotees are equal, regardless of their material wealth or social standing.

To conclude, the story surrounding Sudama's act of presenting a handful of rice to Krishna and Krishna's gracious response to this offering is a deeply moving narrative that perfectly embodies the core ideals of unblemished affection, camaraderie, and genuine acts of benevolence. The story segment in question delves deeper than a mere exchange of gifts; Sudama's offering and Krishna's gracious acceptance serve as enduring symbols, reminding us of the true value of gifts given and received with love and sincerity. The primary message of this narrative is to motivate us to go beyond our focus on materialistic measures and instead, embrace the essence of purity and sincerity that serve as the building blocks for deep relationships and spiritual connections.

Concluding Thoughts: Embracing the Essence of True Friendship

When exploring the intricate fabric of Hindu mythology, one cannot overlook the remarkable account of Krishna and Sudama, a shining embodiment of profound friendship that transcends the ages and serves as a timeless source of wisdom. Within the pages of "Sudama's Friendship: The Riches of Humility and Generosity," readers are invited to delve into the depths of this profound tale, uncovering the nuanced layers of their bond and the virtues it symbolizes. The conclusion of the story skillfully brings together the many threads, emphasizing the timeless lessons it presents and the profound impact it has on our comprehension of friendship, humility, and generosity.

The Timeless Lessons of Krishna and Sudama's Story

The story of Krishna and Sudama, in its very essence, serves as a powerful testament to the immense strength and unblemished nature of genuine friendship. Rather than being based on the conventional indicators of wealth and status, it is rooted in the profound emotions of love, respect, and mutual understanding.

The friendship between them defies the conventional boundaries that society has established. In a society where interpersonal connections are often shaped by financial success and social status, the relationship between Krishna and Sudama serves as a shining example of a genuine bond that goes beyond these shallow confines.

The enduring nature of their relationship, which has been maintained over a significant period and through various stages of life, serves as a powerful reminder that genuine friendships are not fleeting but enduring commitments that endure the trials of time and changing situations.

The Virtues of Humility and Generosity

Sudama, who exemplifies humility, teaches us the importance of gracefully accepting and finding contentment in our circumstances. Him not feeling envious or resentful, even though he is poor, highlights the power that genuine humility possesses.

Krishna's generosity towards Sudama goes far beyond just material possessions. The act of being generous reflects one's spirit and showcases the concept that genuine giving involves comprehending and addressing the needs of others with empathy, all with no expectations of reciprocation.

In the narrative, there is a clear emphasis on valuing spiritual richness over material wealth. The act of Sudama offering humble rice to Krishna and Krishna's magnanimous response serve as a perfect example of how in genuine friendships, emotional and spiritual bonds are more valuable than material transactions.

Embracing the Values in Contemporary Life

In the present-day society that is heavily influenced by wealth and social status, the tale of Krishna and Sudama serves as a reminder for us to reconsider and redefine these notions. The message here is that we should place greater importance on the riches of the heart and spirit, rather than giving significance solely to material possessions and societal labels.

The story they share serves as a powerful reminder that friendships thrive on the foundation of unconditional love and support. One of the valuable lessons it imparts is the importance of extending help and understanding unconditionally, serving as a steadfast pillar of support for our friends during challenging times.

By exploring the narrative, we are motivated to develop deeper and more meaningful human connections, rooted in mutual respect, understanding, and shared values. The encouragement to look beyond external appearances allows us to connect on a deeper level with the intrinsic qualities of individuals.

The Spiritual and Moral Dimensions

The friendship between Krishna and Sudama serves as a powerful example of how relationships can serve as a catalyst for spiritual growth and enlightenment. By showcasing the influence of friendships, we can witness the transformative impact they have on our individual selves and spiritual journeys.

Not only is the story interesting, but it also raises important moral and ethical questions. By advocating for virtues like kindness, selflessness, and empathy, it urges us to include these qualities actively in our interactions and daily routines.

The story of Krishna and Sudama holds within it the incredible ability to shape and impact both social and personal values, fostering a world wherein relationships thrive upon the foundation of genuine intentions, unwavering support, and empathetic understanding.

To conclude, "Sudama's Friendship: The Riches of Humility and Generosity" not only recounts the legendary friendship between Krishna and Sudama, but also offers a profound exploration into the fundamental nature of genuine companionship. The story they shared, with its profound lessons of humility, generosity, and the spiritual aspects of human connections, continues to serve as a timeless symbol of the moral and spiritual abundance that forms the foundation of authentic relationships. This narrative has the remarkable ability to resonate with people of all ages, cultures, and societies, consistently reminding us of the essential values that should shape our interactions and friendships. By embracing the lessons conveyed through the story of Krishna and Sudama, we can enrich our lives on a profound level that extends far beyond the boundaries of material possessions. In doing so, we can foster relationships that are deeply rooted in love, respect, and selflessness - qualities that serve as genuine indicators of lasting and meaningful connections.

Chapter Six

Chapter 6: Dance of the Flute

THE ART OF SUBTLE INFLUENCE

Introduction to Krishna's Artistic Expression

Krishna, in Hindu mythology, is deeply respected and recognized as an embodiment of divine artistry. The life and actions of this individual transcend mere temporal events; they are instead profound artistic expressions imbued with rich spiritual and symbolic significance.

The mesmerizing flute playing and enchanting dance of Krishna are well known, and these artistic talents form an integral aspect of his divine persona. The artistic expressions depicted in these works are not just forms of entertainment, but they are channels through which spiritual truths are manifested, allowing for the transmission of divine influence and evoking deep emotions.

From Krishna's melodious flute playing to his graceful dance movements, every aspect of his artistry carries a profound symbolic significance. These artistic tools serve as a means for Krishna to express messages of love, unity, and spiritual enlightenment.

The Flute as a Symbol of Influence

Within Hindu mythology, the simple bamboo instrument known as Krishna's flute plays a significant role. With its enchanting melodies that have the power to captivate the hearts of anyone who listens, it becomes a symbol of divine charm and influence.

According to legend, the mesmerizing effect of Krishna's flute is said to captivate listeners, bringing them into a state of spiritual ecstasy. It offers a more profound auditory experience by evoking emotions and spiritual connections with the listeners.

The melodies emanating from Krishna's flute serve as a powerful symbol, representing a beckoning to the depths of the soul, and inviting all who listen to embark on a transformative journey towards elevated levels of awareness and spiritual enlightenment. Symbolically, it signifies the divine summoning of the human soul, interesting it to surpass the ordinary and delve into the extraordinary.

Rasleela: The Cosmic Dance

The Rasleela, a divine dance performed by Krishna with the Gopis of Vrindavan, is more than just a dance - it is a profound expression of love and devotion. The significance of this event goes beyond the physical realm, as it represents the spiritual connection between the human soul and the divine.

One of the notable aspects of the Rasleela is its rich use of symbolism. The dance of the universe, the interplay between the divine and the human, and the soul's journey towards union with the absolute are all symbolized by it.

In the Rasleela, an ancient dance performance, Krishna's portrayal involves him joyfully dancing with many Gopis at once. The sight of this enchanting dance performance evokes a sense of divine presence, emphasizing the profound connection between every soul and the d ivine.This aspect of the dance showcases the art of influence through the exuberant expressions of joy, love, and transcendence.

The Rasleela goes beyond being a mere physical expression; it is a profound journey that encompasses emotional and spiritual elevation. The act of dancing, whether actively taking part or merely observing, is said to bring about emotional purification, spiritual upliftment, and a heightened connection with the divine for those involved.

To sum up, the artistic manifestations of Krishna, particularly through the melodious notes of his flute and the captivating Rasleela dance, are remarkable demonstrations of the art of subtle persuasion and deep emotional understanding within the realm of Hindu mythology. The artistic endeavors associated with Krishna's persona are not limited to aesthetics; they carry immense spiritual significance and serve as effective channels for conveying divine love, unity, and spiritual truths. The melodies produced by the flute, combined with the graceful dance movements of the Rasleela, transcend the realm of mere entertainment, reaching deep into the hearts and souls of individuals, ultimately leading them towards a profound spiritual enlightenment. Through his artistry, Krishna creates a sublime harmony of beauty, emotion, and spirituality, affecting individuals on a profound level and fostering a deep connection with them.

The Art of Influence Through Music

Lord Krishna's flute playing in Hindu mythology beautifully illustrates the concept of influence on music, delving deep into the extraordinary ability of music to emotionally connect, transcend boundaries, and appeal universally. The flute in the story of Krishna serves multiple purposes - not only as a musical instrument but also as a symbol of divine influence, capable of eliciting intense emotions and profoundly affecting the soul. This comprehensive exploration delves into the various dimensions of Krishna's musical influence, carefully examining how his flute playing surpasses conventional communication and has a universal appeal that touches the hearts of all beings.

Music as a Medium of Emotional Connection

The reason Krishna's flute playing is so well-known is because it has the remarkable ability to evoke a deep emotional response. His flute produces melodies that are more than just a sequence of notes.

Krishna's flute resonates with such enchanting melodies. It possesses the extraordinary capability to stir the depths of one's inner being, evoking a wide spectrum of feelings from profound longing to sheer euphoria. By serving as a bridge, it can transport listeners from the ordinary to the extraordinary, connecting them with a realm that is both spiritual and profound, offering a heightened sense of consciousness and emotional depth.

According to beliefs, the melodies produced by Krishna have the power to evoke a deep sense of spiritual yearning within those who hear them. Through their music, they can evoke a profound sense of longing for the divine and a strong yearning to merge with the universal consciousness, resulting in listeners often experiencing states of spiritual ecstasy.

Transcending Words and Intellect

Krishna's music has the power to go beyond the limitations of language and intellect, making its influence universal. Unlike words, which are limited by the boundaries of language and logic, music possesses the remarkable ability to address with our innermost being and touch our hearts and souls.

The flute played by Krishna serves as a powerful example of how art, specifically music, can wield greater influence than verbal communication or logical persuasion. One of the remarkable qualities of music is its ability to bypass the logical thinking process and directly connect with a person's emotional and spiritual dimensions.

The reason Krishna's music is so appealing is because it can effectively communicate the universal language of emotion. Its impact goes beyond cultural and linguistic boundaries, as it taps into fundamental human emotions and experiences.

Universal Appeal and Accessibility

That Krishna's flute music has a universal appeal serves as a testament to the inclusive nature of his influence. It extends its reach to individuals, regardless of their social standing, intellectual abilities, or level of spiritual development.

It is said that Krishna's music can attract not just humans, but all beings, including animals and even nature itself. That music is a universal language that transcends species and different life is highlighted by this universal appeal.

Krishna's flute produces such enchanting melodies. They can dismantle the barriers between different social groups and elevate one's spiritual connection. This event can touch the hearts of people from all walks of life, including kings, commoners, the learned, the simple, the spiritually advanced, and even novices. Music's ability to be universally appreciated underscores its capacity to bring people together.

The Transformative Power of Music

The melodious tunes emanating from Krishna's flute possess an extraordinary ability to bring about a profound transformation in those who listen. One of the remarkable things about it is its ability to alter states of consciousness, elevate moods, and even bring about spiritual awakening.

Krishna's music, aside from its spiritual influence, is also renowned for its healing and soothing properties. It is commonly portrayed as having the power to bring a sense of peace and tranquility to troubled hearts and minds that are troubled.

Through the enchanting melodies he plays, Krishna conveys the boundless love and joy that live within the realm of the divine. Their actions and existence are a direct reflection of the cosmic dance of creation, maintenance, and dissolution, vibrating in harmony with the very essence of the universe.

The Flute as a Symbol of Divine Connectivity

According to Hindu mythology, Krishna's flute is viewed as an integral part of his identity, symbolizing his connection to the divine. Through this instrument, he is able to bridge the gap between the earthly and celestial realms by conveying his divine message.

The symbolic nature of the bamboo flute is evident in its selection. The representation of the ideal state of being is made from a simple, hollow bamboo reed, which signifies being empty of ego and pride, enabling it to channel divine energy and produce beautiful music.

In conclusion, it can be said that the art of influence on music, as exemplified by Krishna's mesmerizing flute playing, encompasses deep spiritual and emotional aspects. Through its enchanting melodies, the flute surpasses mere words and intellectual debates, forging a direct connection with the emotions and innermost being. These symbols have the power to communicate a universal language, expressing emotions of love, unity, and spiritual longing that surpass all boundaries, including those of status, intellect, and even species. By employing music to influence, Krishna exemplifies the profound impact that art can have on fostering connections, instilling inspiration, and effecting profound personal change. This concept emphasizes the idea that genuine influence originates from the ability to deeply connect with others on emotional and spiritual levels, thus creating a bond that exceeds the ordinary and brings both the artist and the listener to a heightened level of comprehension and connection.

Rasleela: A Metaphor for Emotional Intelligence

Among the various elements of Hindu mythology, the Rasleela occupies a significant place, symbolizing emotional intelligence through its transformative dance that facilitates spiritual enlightenment and emotional bonding. The participation of Lord Krishna in the Rasleela with the Gopis of Vrindavan goes beyond being a mere narrative of divine play. In this extensive exploration, we delve deep into the Rasleela, using it as a metaphor for emotional intelligence. We meticulously examine its multifaceted aspects and the profound lessons it imparts.

Understanding and Resonating with Emotions

The Rasleela, which is portrayed in Hindu mythology, holds a significance that surpasses its mere portrayal as a dance. This representation, which is mystical and symbolic, showcases Krishna's profound grasp of human emotions. The divine dance that is being performed is a beautiful expression of emotional depth, as it showcases Krishna's incredible ability to connect with and mirror the various emotional states experienced by the Gopis.

Krishna's deep empathy and understanding are beautifully exemplified through his participation in the Rasleela. He can establish a deep emotional connection with every Gopi, acknowledging and addressing their unique emotional needs and states. The deep emotional connection that exists during the Rasleela is what takes it beyond being a mere dance and transforms it into a spiritually uplifting experience.

In the Rasleela, Krishna's role encompasses more than just dancing; he also takes on the responsibility of guiding the Gopis towards a deeper spiritual awakening. Through the art of dance, he leads them on an immersive experience where they embark on a path of emotional and spiritual awakening, showcasing the potency of emotions in navigating one's spiritual journey.

Leadership Through Emotional Connection

The way Krishna leads in the Rasleela serves as a remarkable illustration of how emotional intelligence can be effectively used in leadership. Instead of relying on authority or command, he establishes his influence by demonstrating empathy, understanding, and establishing emotional connections with others.

The way Krishna interacts with the Gopis during the Rasleela is a simple demonstration of his qualities as a leader who is empathetic and understanding. He possesses a remarkable ability to understand and resonate with the emotions of the Gopis, offering them a compassionate and uplifting response.

The Rasleela highlights Krishna's leadership approach, which underscores the value of fostering robust emotional relationships. His ability to create an atmosphere of trust and emotional safety enables him to promote a strong sense of unity and harmony among the individuals involved.

Creating a Shared Emotional Experience

As a quintessential example of how people can come together and create a shared emotional experience, the Rasleela, a traditional dance form, serves. The participants, who come from diverse emotional backgrounds, find common ground in experiencing a collective state of ecstasy. The shared experience we are discussing serves as a powerful illustration, highlighting the impact communal emotional experiences can have in fostering a sense of unity and harmony among individuals.

Through the art of dance, we can express and embody the universal human emotions of joy, sorrow, longing, and fulfillment. The key concept being conveyed is that when individuals share emotional experiences, the impact can be deeply profound, and these experiences can form the foundation for strong communal bonds.

Influence Through Emotional Resonance: Krishna's ability to create and share in these emotional experiences shows an advanced form of influence – one that is based on emotional resonance rather than intellectual persuasion or physical force.

Emotional Intelligence in Personal Growth

One of the profound meanings behind the Rasleela is its representation of the transformative process of self-discovery and emotional evolution. Through their many interactions with Krishna, the Gopis embark on a transformative journey where they gain a deep understanding of their own emotions, leading to significant growth on both personal and spiritual levels.

Through the medium of dance, the Gopis are provided with a means to examine and reflect upon their inner emotional experiences. This enables them to embark on a journey of self-discovery, where they can delve into and comprehend their feelings, desires, and spiritual aspirations.

The Rasleela has the power to become a form of emotional catharsis for many participants. By providing a safe and spiritually uplifting environment, it gives them an opportunity to express and experience their deepest emotions.

The Rasleela as a Universal Metaphor

Although the Rasleela is rooted in Hindu mythology, it goes beyond cultural and religious boundaries. Over time, it takes on a greater meaning, symbolizing the universal strength found in emotional intelligence, empathy, and the shared emotional journeys we all go through.

The lessons derived from the Rasleela apply and significant across a range of contemporary situations, including but not limited to leadership development, team-building exercises, fostering personal relationships, and promoting community engagement. This statement highlights how important it is to possess emotional intelligence in forming meaningful and influential connections.

The Rasleela, a traditional dance form, has served as a profound source of inspiration for many artistic and cultural expressions, with each interpretation seeking to capture the profound emotional and spiritual meaning inherent in the dance. Artists, thinkers, and spiritual seekers are continuously inspired by it, which speaks to its enduring appeal and relevance.

In summary, the comprehensive analysis presented in "Rasleela: A Metaphor for Emotional Intelligence" offers a nuanced and diverse examination of Krishna's part in the Rasleela, shedding light on its symbolic representation of emotional intelligence. The Rasleela is a prime illustration of how individuals who possess a profound comprehension of emotions, exhibit empathetic leadership, and foster shared emotional experiences can effectively bring about spiritual upliftment, communal harmony, and personal growth. This teaches us a valuable lesson about the significance of forming emotional connections with others and the immense power that these connections have in guiding, influencing, and enriching our lives. By being a timeless metaphor, the Rasleela serves to remind us of the profound impact that emotional intelligence can have on our personal journeys and our interactions with the world.

Lessons in Subtle Influence

Lord Krishna's mastery of the art of influence, which mainly involves music and dance, stands as a remarkable illustration of the delicate yet profound power of persuasion found within the intricate realm of Hindu mythology. Not only does he excel in these arts, but his mastery goes beyond simply providing entertainment. The exploration titled "Lessons in Subtle Influence" takes a thorough analysis of the complex and diverse ways in which Krishna's influence is manifested. It thoroughly examines how this influence is expressed through various forms of art, music, dance, as well as emotional intelligence. It explores the valuable lessons that can be derived from Krishna's influence in the realms of leadership, communication, and interpersonal connections.

Influence Without Coercion

Emotional connectivity forms the foundation of Krishna's approach to influence, emphasizing the importance of establishing deep connections with others. His involvement in the Rasleela and his exceptional flute playing skills are not just artistic pursuits, but they are means of exerting a subtle yet potent influence. They serve as an example of how genuine influence is attained by resonating with others emotionally, rather than relying on coercion or obvious persuasion tactics.

The influence of Krishna is focused on subtly guiding individuals towards the emotional or spiritual state they desire. By his music and dance, he effectively establishes a connection with the emotions of individuals, guiding them subtly towards transformative encounters of spiritual enlightenment, happiness, and self-discovery.

The Power of Art in Communication

The utilization of music and dance by Krishna serves to emphasize the significant role of art in effective communication. The various forms of art possess the remarkable capacity to communicate intricate emotions and ideas that often surpass the limitations of traditional spoken language.

Krishna's music and dance serve as a powerful example of how art can transcend cultural, linguistic, and intellectual boundaries, emphasizing the notion that art is a universal language. Its ability to address to the heart gives it a powerful advantage as a means of communication and influence.

The stories Krishna tells through his art are both emotional and spiritual. Through the enchanting melodies of his flute and the meticulously synchronized movements of the Rasleela, meaningful messages of divine love, the cosmic dance, and the harmonious connection between souls and the divine are portrayed.

Emotional Intelligence in Leadership

The interactions between Krishna and the Gopis during the Rasleela showcase a remarkable level of emotional intelligence. With his acute awareness of the Gopis' emotional states, he can respond to them with empathy and understanding, displaying a remarkable level of emotional intelligence.

Krishna's remarkable ability to empathize with the Gopis, demonstrating a deep understanding and a willingness to share in their emotional experiences, serves as an interesting illustration of effective, empathetic leadership. With the Rasleela, his leadership style is not centered on authority or dominance, but focuses on establishing emotional connections and fostering mutual understanding.

Krishna's demonstration emphasizes the idea that successful leadership includes the ability to emotionally connect with those being led. Leaders can inspire, motivate, and influence their followers in a way that is not only profound but also has a lasting impact when they take such action.

The Subtlety of Influence through Art

When examining Krishna's use of music and dance to influence, one can observe a fascinating study in subtlety. Rather than dictating or commanding, he communicates indirectly.

The reason Krishna's influence is elegant is that it operates indirectly. By expressing himself artistically, he creates a space for individuals to interpret and internalize messages, thereby fostering self-reflection and facilitating personal growth.

The Rasleela is more than just a dance between Krishna and the Gopis; it is about the creation of a shared experience. Through the participation of everyone in the dance, a sense of collective involvement is fostered, leading to an emotional and spiritual journey that highlights the influence of shared experiences.

Art and Emotional Intelligence in Modern Contexts

In modern leadership contexts, the relevance of Krishna's subtle influence on art and emotional intelligence cannot be overstated. There are several valuable lessons that today's leaders can learn from Krishna's example, such as the significance of empathy, establishing emotional connections, and using creative methods to inspire and influence others.

In today's modern era where communication is predominantly confined to verbal and written means, Krishna's artistic abilities serve as a poignant reminder of the profound impact that non-verbal forms of communication, such as music, art, and dance, can have in effectively conveying intricate concepts and profound emotions, as well as establishing meaningful connections with others.

By observing Krishna's interactions, one can easily recognize the significance of nurturing emotional intelligence in both personal and professional domains. By cultivating a genuine understanding and empathy towards the emotions of those around us, we can foster stronger and more meaningful relationships, while also becoming more effective leaders.

In summary, "Lessons in Subtle Influence" provides an in-depth exploration of how Krishna's utilization of music, dance, and emotional intelligence as tools for influence imparts profound insights applicable to communication, leadership, and interpersonal relationships. The teachings of Krishna highlight the importance of emotional connection, using art as a universal language for communication, and leading others with empathy and profound understanding as the key components of true influence. The lessons provided have stood the test of time and remain highly relevant, offering valuable guidance on how to subtly and effectively influence different aspects of life, including personal relationships and professional leadership.

Conclusion: Embracing Artistic Influence and Emotional Intelligence

Among the many captivating stories and legends found within Hindu mythology, "Dance of the Flute: The Art of Subtle Influence" emerges as a remarkable and thought-provoking exploration into the intricate realm of Lord Krishna's utilization of music and dance. It delves beyond the realm of mere artistic expression and uncovers their profound potential as influential tools and channels for imparting emotional intelligence. With his mesmerizing flute melodies and the ethereal Rasleela, Krishna showcases an extraordinary level of artistry that extends beyond the confines of the physical world, leaving a profound impact on the hearts and souls of all who have the privilege of experiencing it. In the conclusion of this chapter, we explore how Krishna's artistic expressions serve as valuable lessons in subtle influence, fostering emotional connection, and highlighting the crucial role of emotional intelligence in effective leadership.

The Multifaceted Power of Krishna's Artistry

The way Krishna incorporates music and dance showcases the power of art as an influential tool. The flute melodies produced by him and the Rasleela are more than just mere entertainments;

In the hands of Krishna, the flute transforms into a powerful symbol, embodying both divine allure and emotional resonance, while the Rasleela vividly portrays the cosmic interplay between the human and the divine. These artistic expressions contain deep insights into various aspects of life, including spirituality and the fundamental nature of human connections.

Krishna's exceptional emotional intelligence shines through in his interactions within these artistic endeavors, placing him at the forefront. With his innate ability to understand, empathize with, and influence the emotional states of others, he guides them towards spiritual and emotional enlightenment, showcasing his remarkable talents.

Lessons in Subtle Influence

One of the main takeaways from Krishna's artistry is the remarkable ability to influence others through non-verbal means. Through his mesmerizing flute playing and active involvement in the Rasleela, he exerts a profound influence that transcends verbal expression, touching the very depths of the hearts and souls of those who listen and take part.

The influence of Krishna is known for its subtlety and indirectness, which sets it apart. His approach is to not impose or assert his will, which sets him apart from others.

The artistry of Krishna serves as a testament to the effectiveness of communication without words. The depth of the emotions and messages that he conveys through his music and dance is truly profound, serving as a powerful reminder that non-verbal communication can be incredibly impactful.

The Role of Emotional Intelligence in Leadership

The manner in which Krishna performs during the Rasleela can be seen as an ideal representation of empathetic leadership. With his remarkable ability to connect with people on a profound emotional level, he not only understands their individual emotional needs but also responds to them, ultimately leading them towards a state of collective euphoria and spiritual awakening.

The way Krishna can emotionally connect with those around him emphasizes the importance of emotional resonance as a vital skill in effective leadership. By adopting this style of leadership, a stronger bond and mutual comprehension are cultivated between the leader and the followers, ultimately resulting in a more unified and motivated approach to action.

Krishna's leadership approach serves as a prime example of how one can effectively integrate both the emotional and rational dimensions in the decision-making process. In his demonstration, he shows that effective leadership requires more than just logical reasoning; it also causes a profound comprehension and active involvement in emotional dynamics.

Embracing Art and Emotional Intelligence in Modern Life

In the present day, the lessons derived from Krishna's utilization of music and dance remain highly pertinent. In today's modern era where digital communication frequently takes precedence over face-to-face interactions, the significance of emotional intelligence, empathy, and the delicate intricacies of non-verbal communication are particularly emphasized.

Krishna's artistry serves as a catalyst, inspiring and motivating us to delve into the world of art, recognizing its potential as a powerful tool for both personal and professional development. Engaging with art, whether it be through music, dance, or other art forms, has the incredible potential to enhance various aspects of our lives, such as our emotional intelligence, communication skills, and ability to positively influence others.

In the narrative, there is a powerful encouragement to foster emotional intelligence by focusing on skills like empathy, emotional awareness, and the ability to establish emotional connections with others. The importance of these skills extends beyond leadership; they help to nurture significant personal relationships and promoting a society that embraces empathy.

To conclude, "Dance of the Flute: The Art of Subtle Influence" serves as a guide that stands the test of time, showcasing the deep influence of artistic expression and emotional intelligence in the domain of leadership and influence. Through Krishna's incorporation of music and dance, he surpasses the boundaries of mere artistic expression, delving into the profound realm of understanding the art of subtle manipulation and the immense impact of emotional resonance. The narrative serves as a source of inspiration, urging us to embrace these dimensions in our personal lives, acknowledging the transformative power of art to foster deep communication, forge soulful connections, and ignite profound inspiration within hearts and minds. During the intricate challenges posed by modern life, the teachings derived from Krishna's flute and the Rasleela serve as guiding lights, leading us towards a life that is more empathetic, emotionally intelligent, and artistically enriched.

Chapter Seven

Chapter 7: Govinda's Guidance

Leading with Compassion and Wisdom

Lord Krishna, amidst the captivating richness of Hindu mythology, arises as a remarkable symbol of exemplary divine leadership. He is known by the name Govinda and is highly respected not only for his divine qualities but also for his extensive wisdom, profound compassion, and ability to excel in various leadership positions. Entitled "Krishna's Leadership Persona," this comprehensive exploration thoroughly explores the multifaceted dimensions of Krishna's leadership. It meticulously analyzes how his distinctive fusion of qualities establishes him as an exemplary leader in different domains, encompassing spirituality, politics, and society.

Krishna's Leadership Persona

Krishna, or Govinda, embodies an ideal leadership persona that is a harmonious blend of divine attributes. He is a figure of immense power and wisdom, yet he is approachable and compassionate, making him an extraordinary leader.

When it comes to Krishna's leadership, one of the most remarkable aspects is the perfect combination of compassion and wisdom that he possesses. With a heart filled with understanding and a mind full of wisdom, he takes the lead, skillfully balancing emotional intelligence and practical insight.

Krishna's approachable nature beautifully complements his divine prowess. One of the key aspects of his leadership is his accessibility, which extends to individuals from all walks of life, ranging from the most humble to the highest positions.

Multidimensional Leadership Role

Across a wide range of realms, Krishna assumes a prominent role as a leader. He exhibits leadership in various domains, showcasing his expertise as a spiritual guide, a wise statesman, a master strategist in warfare, and a compassionate friend and mentor, rather than being confined to just one area.

Krishna, in his capacity as a spiritual guide, imparts deeply insightful and profound philosophical as well as spiritual teachings, which are particularly highlighted in the Bhagavad Gita. When it comes to spiritual matters, his guidance extends beyond religious practices and delves into the profound understanding of life's deeper truths.

Krishna, known for his role in the Mahabharata, showcases exceptional political acumen and strategic foresight, establishing himself as a remarkable statesman and strategist. The way he provides guidance and advice in both political and warfare situations is a clear indication of his deep understanding of intricate socio-political dynamics.

Krishna is not only admired for his divine qualities, but he is also highly regarded as a compassionate friend and mentor. In his interactions with a wide range of individuals, including the Pandavas as well as the common people, he consistently demonstrates his remarkable qualities of empathy, understanding, and the capacity to provide guidance to others with both kindness and wisdom.

Leadership Through Compassion

Krishna's leadership style is characterized by a deep-rooted sense of empathy. With his deep understanding and ability to connect with others, he guides them through their emotions and struggles, offering compassion and empathy.

Acts of kindness and understanding are often the ways through which Krishna's influence is exerted. Through his compassionate actions and words, he leads by inspiring trust and respect among others.

Krishna's decisions, even when faced with challenging circumstances, are always guided by a deep sense of compassion. Taking into account the well-being of all individuals involved, he strives to find a harmonious equilibrium between the principles of justice and mercy.

Leadership Through Wisdom

Both insight and visionary thinking are qualities that define Krishna's wisdom. His knowledge extends to a profound understanding of not only the human condition but also the laws of nature and the intricate workings of the universe.

One of Krishna's notable attributes is his strategic thinking and his proficiency in solving complex problems. One of his notable qualities is his ability to come up with innovative solutions that not only tackle the underlying issues but also take into consideration the broader consequences of his actions.

Krishna's advice is invaluable in complex situations as it combines practicality with a strong moral foundation. His clarity and insight make him an invaluable resource in helping individuals navigate through moral dilemmas and ethical quandaries.

Balancing Emotional and Rational Aspects

The way Krishna leads is a perfect demonstration of how to achieve a harmonious balance between the heart and the mind. The point he makes is that successful leadership entails the ability to balance emotional intelligence with rational thinking.

One of the defining characteristics of Krishna's leadership style is his ability to adapt and be flexible. His adaptability is evident as he is able to modify his approach according to the context and needs of the situation, all the while upholding his core values of wisdom and compassion.

In conclusion, it can be stated that Krishna's portrayal of Govinda showcases the qualities of an ideal leader. The comprehensive model of effective leadership that he offers is a result of his unique combination of divine attributes, profound wisdom, deep compassion, and versatile leadership roles across various facets of life and mythology. Krishna's demonstration highlights the importance of leading with empathy and understanding, making wise decisions through insight and wisdom, and influencing others positively with kindness and compassion. His leadership style illuminates the path for leaders across various domains, inspiring them to lead with a harmonious balance of heart and mind, empathy and strategic thinking, and compassion and wisdom.

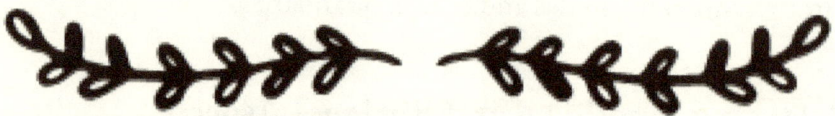

Compassion in Leadership

When it comes to leadership, compassion is a fundamental aspect that serves as a crucial foundation for both effective and ethical guidance. Lord Krishna, who is considered a central figure in Hindu mythology, demonstrates this virtue through his multifaceted role as a leader, mentor, and guide. The leadership style that he exhibits is characterized by a deep sense of empathy, making compassionate decisions, and using kindness as a means of influence, which provides invaluable lessons on how to lead with a compassionate heart. In this comprehensive exploration, we delve deep into the numerous facets of Krishna's compassionate leadership, thoroughly examining how his approach not only affects the immediate circumstances but also makes a lasting impact on the broader spectrum of society and morality.

Empathy and Understanding

A deep-seated empathy and understanding form the foundation of Krishna's leadership. Rather than leading with authority, he chooses to lead with compassion, establishing connections with individuals on an emotional and spiritual level.

Krishna possesses a deep understanding that surpasses mere surface-level emotions and situations. With great insight and empathy, he is able to perceive the deeper emotional currents and spiritual dilemmas of those he guides, providing guidance and support accordingly.

The fact that Krishna possesses such a deep understanding is a clear manifestation of his high emotional intelligence. Through his adeptness, he is able to accurately interpret emotions, grasp their meanings, and then provide compassionate and enlightening responses.

Compassionate Decision Making

When making decisions, Krishna takes into account both strategic soundness and moral considerations, striking a delicate balance between the two. His decision-making process remains steadfastly rooted in compassion, even when faced with the most arduous of circumstances, as he considers both the greater good and the ethical implications at hand.

Krishna's decisions in different narratives, including the Mahabharata, showcase his exceptional foresight in comprehending the lasting consequences of his actions, not only on individuals but also on the overall societal structure.

The leadership style he exhibits emphasizes the crucial role that moral and ethical considerations play in decision-making. Krishna's actions serve as a testament to the idea that effective leadership requires skillfully maneuvering through complex situations while upholding values of compassion and ethics.

Influencing with Kindness

Krishna sets himself apart from leaders who resort to fear or authority by employing the power of kindness and benevolence to influence others. His interactions with people are defined by a heartfelt and genuine concern for the well-being of others.

Krishna's guidance, particularly in matters related to spirituality and life, is characterized by a nurturing and compassionate approach that is truly remarkable. His leadership style involves guiding individuals towards personal growth and enlightenment, using gentle persuasion and compassionate guidance instead of coercion.

By adopting the approach of leading with kindness, Krishna is able to cultivate a strong sense of trust and respect among his followers.

This leadership style not only establishes influence but also endears those who follow it.

Compassionate Leadership in Various Roles

The compassionate nature of Krishna shines through as he fulfills his role as a spiritual guide, providing guidance and solutions to individuals grappling with spiritual doubts and dilemmas. By offering guidance that is both compassionate and enlightening, he supports individuals in unraveling the complexities of the spiritual maze, enabling them to find their way.

The role of Krishna in the Mahabharata is not only significant in political and social contexts, but it also showcases his compassionate approach. When advocating for justice and righteousness, he consistently maintains a compassionate and understanding perspective towards the human condition.

Whether Krishna is interacting with friends like Arjuna or with ordinary individuals, his mentorship is firmly based on compassion in his personal interactions. His understanding of personal struggles allows him to provide guidance that is both practical and empathetic to those in need.

Challenges and Resolutions in Compassionate Leadership

Krishna's life is full of various instances in which he finds himself confronted with difficult choices, frequently entailing conflicts and moral quandaries. The approach he takes in these particular situations gives us valuable insights into how leaders who possess compassion can effectively navigate challenging decisions.

When faced with conflicts, Krishna frequently chooses compassion as a method for resolving them. In his quest for resolution, he makes a conscious effort to seek fair and just solutions that also demonstrate empathy and understanding towards all parties involved.

Krishna's leadership is especially evident in times of crisis, as it showcases the immense power of compassion to alleviate fears, foster resilience, and navigate through turbulent situations with a renewed sense of hope and reassurance.

The Ripple Effect of Compassionate Leadership

The compassionate leadership of Krishna not only affects the immediate context but also has a profound impact on broader societal values. The way he approaches things fosters an environment that values empathy, understanding, and ethical behavior.

Krishna's style of leadership is seen as an inspiration for upcoming leaders. This particular example serves to demonstrate how taking a compassionate approach can contribute to the development of a society that is more humane and guided by ethical principles.

Krishna's leadership has left a lasting legacy that goes beyond the constraints of time, providing valuable lessons that remain applicable throughout different eras. The approach he takes has the power to inspire leaders from different fields to incorporate compassion as a fundamental element of their leadership style.

To conclude, the concept of "Compassion in Leadership" as demonstrated by Krishna provides deep understanding of the skill of guiding others with empathy, kindness, and wisdom. His leadership persona, which is defined by a profound comprehension, empathetic decision-making, and a gentle influence, serves as a model in the domains of spiritual, political, and social leadership. The importance of compassion in leadership is emphasized by this exploration, which demonstrates how having a heart full of empathy and understanding can result in decisions that are not only strategically sound but also morally and ethically elevated. Krishna's leadership style is not only an inspiration for current and future leaders but also a reminder to prioritize compassion as an essential aspect of effective and ethical leadership.

Wisdom in Leadership

Within Hindu mythology, Lord Krishna's leadership is renowned for its wisdom, as it harmoniously combines spiritual insights with practical understanding. His wisdom, which is illustrated in a multitude of texts and narratives, especially in the Bhagavad Gita, showcases an exceptional ability to provide guidance that is both deeply spiritual and highly practical. This in-depth exploration thoroughly examines and delves into various aspects of Krishna's profound wisdom and its application in the realm of leadership. By exploring his role in the

Bhagavad Gita and the Mahabharata, the book demonstrates how his teachings and strategies have enduring relevance in the realm of effective leadership.

Profound Spiritual and Practical Wisdom

The wisdom possessed by Krishna is a rare combination of profound spirituality and practical intelligence. The teachings and decisions made by him are a clear demonstration of his profound comprehension of spiritual truths, which he adeptly utilizes in practical scenarios.

The wisdom that Krishna possesses is not confined to either the spiritual or the material aspects; it transcends both. His guidance is not limited to spiritual growth; it extends to the practicalities of daily life, governance, and warfare as well.

One of the notable strengths that Krishna demonstrates as a wise leader is his skill in finding a delicate equilibrium between idealistic spiritual principles and the practical aspects of human life. By acknowledging the intricacies of life, he presents solutions that effectively navigate these complexities while upholding ethical principles.

The Bhagavad Gita: A Testament to Krishna's Wisdom

The Bhagavad Gita, which is a dialogue between Krishna and Arjuna, stands as a powerful testament to the immense wisdom possessed by Krishna. Within the pages of this sacred text, Krishna shares profound teachings on various subjects including duty (dharma), righteousness, the intricacies of life and death, and the different paths that lead to spiritual liberation.

In the context of the Gita, we find ourselves on a battlefield, witnessing Arjuna's struggle with a profound moral and existential crisis. The guidance that Krishna provides in this critical moment extends far beyond the immediate scenario, encompassing lessons that are universally applicable and will remain relevant throughout time.

In the Gita, Krishna's wisdom specifically deals with the intricate dynamics between one's duty, personal desires, and morality. He provides guidance to Arjuna, stressing the significance of carrying out one's duty without being attached to the results, and emphasizing the importance of righteous action.

Krishna's wisdom extends to the profound understanding of life, death, the eternal soul (atman), and the fleeting nature of the physical world. By following his teachings, individuals are motivated to embrace a wider viewpoint when facing the obstacles that life throws at them, and to actively pursue spiritual wisdom.

Strategic and Visionary Leadership

In the epic Mahabharata, Krishna's character is portrayed as a prime example of strategic and visionary leadership. His ability to navigate complex political and social landscapes with astute strategies is often the determining factor in shaping the course of events.

Krishna's guidance is distinguished by its emphasis on looking ahead and planning for the future. By anticipating future scenarios and strategically preparing for them, he ensures the welfare of not only individuals but also the broader societal context.

One of Krishna's notable qualities is his well-regarded diplomatic skills and his ability to employ strategic maneuvers. His interventions within the Mahabharata are of great importance, as they have the power to subtly shape key events and outcomes in significant ways.

Krishna's strategic leadership is notably enhanced by his extensive grasp of human psychology. By comprehending the motivations, strengths, and weaknesses of individuals, he is able to effectively guide, counsel, and influence outcomes.

Ethical and Moral Leadership

The leadership of Krishna is characterized by his unwavering dedication to the principles of Dharma, which emphasize righteousness and fulfilling one's duties. His advocacy extends to promoting actions that are both ethically sound and in accordance with the greater good, even in cases where they involve making tough choices.

Krishna's wisdom is particularly evident and shines through when faced with moral complexity. His approach to navigating ethical dilemmas is characterized by a sophisticated understanding, allowing him to provide guidance that harmonizes moral integrity and practical necessity.

The way Krishna approaches leadership can be viewed as a model for ethical leadership. Leaders can learn valuable lessons in managing the ethical complexities of their roles from his actions and decisions, which are guided by wisdom and morality.

The Impact of Krishna's Wisdom on Leadership

The wisdom of Krishna, which is prominently illustrated in both the Gita and the Mahabharata, has a profound and lasting impact on modern interpretations of leadership. His teachings offer valuable insights on how to lead with integrity, strategic foresight, and moral responsibility.

One can find valuable lessons in Krishna's leadership style, which modern leaders can draw upon. These lessons include the significance of ethical decision-making, the need to strike a balance between spiritual insights and practical realities, and the role of strategic thinking in achieving effective leadership.

Krishna's wisdom surpasses the boundaries of conventional leadership practices. This resource provides valuable guidance and insights for individuals looking to enhance personal growth, develop self-awareness, and strive for a well-rounded and purposeful existence.

In summary, "Wisdom in Leadership" perfectly captures the core of Krishna's leadership style, showcasing his exceptional wisdom that encompasses both the spiritual and practical realms. By examining his guidance in the Bhagavad Gita and his strategic role in the Mahabharata, one can uncover valuable lessons on effective leadership that transcend time. Krishna serves as a prime example of how genuine leadership encompasses a combination of ethical integrity, strategic foresight, and a profound comprehension of both human nature and societal dynamics. The teachings of this individual continue to hold significance throughout different time periods, providing valuable perspectives for present-day leaders and individuals who desire to navigate the intricacies of life with both wisdom and moral clarity. When we embrace and put into practice the teachings of Krishna's leadership, we can strive to become leaders who not only achieve results but also experience moral and spiritual growth.

Leading with a Balanced Approach

Lord Krishna's leadership, within the vast and intricate narratives of Hindu mythology, serves as an exceptional example of balance, adaptability, and inspiration. With his ability to seamlessly blend compassion with practical wisdom, his approach to leadership showcases a mastery over the art of leading effectively in varied situations. This detailed exploration takes a closer look at Krishna's leadership approach, highlighting how he skillfully incorporates adaptability, versatility, and inspirational qualities in his roles as a spiritual guide, strategist, and mentor.

Balancing Compassion and Practicality

Krishna's leadership is a shining example of the perfect balance between emotions and intellect. Whether he is guiding individuals on their spiritual journey or strategizing in warfare, his decisions and actions always showcase an impressive equilibrium between profound compassion and shrewd practical wisdom.

With his innate understanding and ability to empathize with others, Krishna is able to effectively navigate complex situations, thanks to his strategic acumen. The way he leads emphasizes the importance of recognizing and comprehending emotions, and utilizing that comprehension to make knowledgeable and strategic choices, thus illustrating that genuine leadership entails this understanding.

When examining different narratives, it becomes evident that Krishna consistently demonstrates a compassionate yet pragmatic approach when making decisions. In his actions, he demonstrates that effective leadership encompasses not only showing concern for the well-being of others, but also having the courage to make difficult decisions that are essential for the betterment of the whole.

Adaptability and Versatility

Adaptability and versatility are prominent features of Krishna's leadership. His versatility is evident as he takes on multiple roles, including a spiritual guide in the Bhagavad Gita, a master strategist in the Mahabharata, and a guiding friend to the Pandavas, among others. Depending on the role and the people involved, he modifies his leadership style to effectively meet the needs of the situation.

One aspect that sets Krishna apart as a leader is his remarkable capacity to adjust and thrive in response to evolving situations. Being flexible and responsive to the dynamics of each situation is an essential skill for any effective leader, and he demonstrates the importance of this skill.

Despite being adaptable, Krishna remains steadfast in his adherence to his core values of wisdom, compassion, and righteousness. The crucial aspect of ensuring effective and ethically sound leadership lies in the consistent adherence to core values.

Inspirational Leadership

Krishna's leadership is characterized by both verbal guidance and setting a positive example for others to follow. His actions, which are defined by qualities such as wisdom, compassion, and integrity, have a profound impact on those who observe him, compelling them to seek out and embody these virtues in their own lives.

Those who are fortunate enough to witness Krishna's leadership are uplifted and motivated by his unique approach. His ability to inspire knows no bounds, as he encourages individuals to strive for greatness and uncover their untapped strengths.

Krishna's impact is not limited to his immediate presence; it extends far and wide due to his actions and the wisdom he imparts. The profound impact of his teachings in the Bhagavad Gita can be seen in the way they continue to inspire and guide millions of people across the globe.

Wisdom and Compassion in Leadership

The deep integration of wisdom is evident in Krishna's decision-making process. In addition to contemplating the immediate consequences of his choices, he also takes into account the long-term ramifications, guaranteeing that his actions are in harmony with a more comprehensive perspective on what is right and beneficial.

Krishna's leadership style serves as a shining example of how compassion can be embraced as a strength, rather than perceived as a weakness. Through his actions, he exemplifies the importance of empathizing with others and comprehending their viewpoints, ultimately leading to decision-making that is more effective and inclusive.

The way Krishna balances diverse interests and perspectives demonstrates his skill in managing complex situations. His ability to navigate through conflicting interests while prioritizing outcomes that benefit all parties involved is commendable.

Challenges and Triumphs in Balanced Leadership

Krishna frequently finds himself in situations where he encounters ethical dilemmas that require him to make difficult decisions. By observing his approach in these situations, one can gain a deeper understanding of how leaders who prioritize balance can successfully navigate ethical complexities without compromising their core values.

Whether it is the familial disputes portrayed in the epic Mahabharata or his wise counsel to Arjuna, Krishna's interventions exemplify his aptitude for conflict resolution, which involves a balanced consideration of both emotional and rational factors.

The effectiveness of a leadership approach that is well-balanced is highlighted by the successes and triumphs of Krishna, whether it be in securing the victory of the Pandavas in the Mahabharata or in imparting timeless wisdom in the Bhagavad Gita.

To summarize, the concept of "Leading with a Balanced Approach" effectively showcases Lord Krishna's leadership style, which is characterized by its multifaceted and nuanced nature. The high standard of leadership is set by his ability to blend compassion with practical wisdom, adapt to various roles while maintaining core values, and inspire others through his actions. Krishna's approach to leadership provides valuable insights for both current leaders and individuals, highlighting the significance of finding a harmonious blend between emotional intelligence and practical decision-making, maintaining a balance between adaptability and consistency, and combining inspiration with strategic action. Leaders and individuals can strive to create a positive impact in their realms of influence by embracing and integrating the elements of Krishna's balanced leadership model. This model allows them to lead in a manner that is not only effective and ethical but also inspiring.

Conclusion: Embracing Krishna's Leadership Qualities

Within the vast and intricate tapestry of Hindu mythology, the majestic figure of Lord Krishna emerges as a towering symbol of exemplary leadership, encapsulating virtues that remain just as pertinent in contemporary times as they did in the age-old epics. In the conclusion of "Govinda's Guidance: Leading with Compassion and Wisdom," the author brings together the key elements of Krishna's leadership, emphasizing the enduring significance of his attributes such as compassion, wisdom, strategic thinking, and spiritual insight. By conducting a comprehensive analysis, it becomes evident that Krishna's leadership style not only serves as a model for effective and ethical leadership, but also offers valuable lessons for individuals across different spheres of life, all while being informed by spirituality.

Synthesis of Krishna's Leadership Model

The leadership model that Krishna follows is a beautiful blend of compassion and wisdom, creating a harmonious integration. When it comes to his approach, he combines a strong sense of empathy and understanding with a strategic foresight and practical decision-making. By using this blend, he is able to skillfully handle complex situations while still maintaining his moral and ethical integrity.

One of the distinguishing factors of Krishna's leadership is his incorporation of spiritual insight, which adds a unique dimension to his approach. He believes that leadership goes beyond being a mere role; it is a solemn duty to inspire and steer others towards greater moral and spiritual values. One can find profound spiritual insights in his teachings, such as those found in the Bhagavad Gita, which transcend the confines of the battlefield.

In the epic Mahabharata, Krishna's role not only demonstrates his strategic thinking abilities, but also highlights his unwavering commitment to upholding ethical standards. In his demonstration, he showcases the essence of true leadership, which encompasses the ability to make difficult decisions that are not only intelligent and impactful, but also fair and morally upright.

Lessons for Modern Leaders and Individuals

There are several significant lessons that modern leaders can learn from Krishna's leadership style. Leaders who embrace empathy and strategic insight have the ability to make decisions that go beyond mere effectiveness, as they take into account compassion and consideration for the broader impact on people and society.

The leadership displayed by Krishna serves as a clear example of the significance of ethical leadership. His model serves as a reminder of the importance of leading with integrity and moral clarity in a world where ethical dilemmas are becoming increasingly complex.

Krishna's leadership style goes beyond simply guiding others; it also encompasses the ability to inspire those around him. The combination of his wisdom, compassion, and actions allows him to effectively influence and motivate others, making him an exceptional role model for inspirational leadership.

Integrating Krishna's Qualities in Contemporary Leadership

The process of embracing Krishna's leadership qualities entails the adoption of a well-rounded approach that harmonizes compassion and practical wisdom. When it comes to decision-making, leaders can aim to find a balance between empathy and consideration on one hand, and strategic thinking and effectiveness on the other.

An important aspect of integrating Krishna's qualities is the promotion of ethical and spiritual growth, which encompasses personal development as well as the growth of others. Leaders have the ability to work towards the creation of environments that foster moral development and promote a greater comprehension of one's obligations and commitments.

Krishna's leadership is motivated by a strong vision that aims to create a positive impact on a larger scale. Modern leaders have the opportunity to emulate this approach by establishing visions that surpass individual or organizational benefits and strive for wider societal and ethical improvement.

In summary, "Govinda's Guidance: Leading with Compassion and Wisdom" encompasses the deep and multifaceted leadership qualities demonstrated by Lord Krishna. With a leadership style that encompasses compassion, wisdom, strategic thinking, and spiritual insight, he offers a timeless roadmap for effective and ethical leadership. By fully embracing and seamlessly integrating these qualities into their leadership approach, contemporary leaders and individuals have the opportunity to aspire to a style of leadership that is not only highly effective in achieving goals, but also deeply enriching in its moral and spiritual dimensions. Krishna's leadership model serves as a constant source of inspiration, providing us with guidance on how to become leaders who are not only successful in their endeavors, but also exhibit qualities of compassion, wisdom, and spiritual awareness. In doing so, we aim to contribute to the creation of a more ethical and enlightened world.

Chapter Eight

Chapter 8: Battlefield Illumination

Embracing Life's Challenges

Context of the Kurukshetra War

The Kurukshetra war, situated within the grand tapestry of the Mahabharata, assumes a pivotal role, going beyond its conventional portrayal as a mere battle, whether in history or mythology, and instead serves as a powerful symbol of the timeless conflict between what is just and unjust, right and wrong. In this extensive exploration, we delve deep into the context of the Kurukshetra war, thoroughly examining its significance and shedding light on the pivotal role played by the divine Lord Krishna. In addition to narrating the events that occurred before and during the war, this section also provides a detailed analysis of the moral and ethical dilemmas that emerged and highlights Krishna's crucial role in guiding the Pandavas, especially Arjuna, during this challenging period.

The Kurukshetra war, which is a pivotal event in the Mahabharata, represents more than just a face-off between two factions. The symbolization of this is rooted in the timeless conflict between dharma, representing righteousness, and adharma, symbolizing unrighteousness. This conflict also represents the battle between justice and injustice.

The epic battle, with its complexities and contradictions, serves as a powerful reflection of the intricate and paradoxical nature that characterizes human society. By representing the moral and ethical struggles that individuals and societies face, it sheds light on the difficult choices and compromises that are frequently encountered as part of the human experience.

The war is the culmination of a long-standing feud between the Pandavas and the Kauravas, two branches of a royal family. The conflict that we are witnessing is deeply entrenched in issues such as greed, envy, familial discord, and the relentless pursuit of power.

Krishna's Pivotal Role

In this magnificent and awe-inspiring setting, Lord Krishna takes on a role that goes far beyond the traditional and usual conventions. His role extends beyond that of a mere participant or charioteer, as he assumes the responsibilities of a guide, philosopher, and strategist. The war's course and outcome are greatly influenced by his presence, making it a pivotal factor.

Krishna's most significant role is as the guide and mentor to Arjuna, the great Pandava warrior. In the midst of the fierce Kurukshetra battlefield, Krishna imparts to Arjuna a profound wisdom that transcends the boundaries of the war itself.

Krishna, throughout the conflict, symbolizes divine wisdom and the cosmic law that governs the universe. His role extends beyond being a moral compass solely for Arjuna; he fulfills this important function for all those who are part of the unfolding events, directing them towards the reestablishment of dharma.

The Precipitation of the War

A complex tapestry of relationships, decisions, and events weaves its way through the lead-up to the Kurukshetra war. From the game of dice to the exile of the Pandavas, each event that unfolds in the Mahabharata serves to intricately build upon the eventual conflict.

The war is initiated due to a sequence of actions characterized by a decline in moral values, rampant injustice, and an insatiable hunger for power exhibited by the Kauravas. Despite numerous attempts at reconciliation, the denial of justice to the Pandavas ultimately paves the way for the unavoidable conflict.

The sequence of events that transpired and eventually led to the war provides a clear illustration of how the divine plan and human actions are intertwined. Even though it seems inevitable that the war will happen, the characters' choices and actions greatly influence its actualization.

The Battle as a Moral and Ethical Arena

In the epic battle of Kurukshetra, the stage is set for the confrontation between dharma, representing virtue and righteousness, and adharma, symbolizing evil and immorality. The battlefield is filled with moral and ethical implications, as each warrior, decision, and action carries great weight.

Krishna's intention in intervening and providing guidance is to maintain the principles of dharma. In his role, he ensures that the Pandavas navigate the moral complexities of the war, steadfastly adhering to the path of righteousness, even though it may be challenging.

The external war serves as a symbol for the internal struggles that every person encounters. The dilemmas and choices that arise on the battlefield serve as a mirror for the inner conflicts that humans wrestle with as they strive for righteousness and justice.

Krishna's Teachings in the Midst of War

In the midst of the chaotic and tumultuous battlefield, Krishna selflessly imparts the timeless and profound teachings of the Bhagavad Gita to a deeply despondent and conflicted Arjuna. With its profound spiritual and moral wisdom, this sacred text emerges as a beacon, offering guidance to both Arjuna and the entirety of humanity.

Krishna, in the Gita, provides insight and guidance on how to navigate the moral dilemmas presented by the war. In his speech, he discusses various topics such as duty, righteousness, the impermanence of life, and the immortality of the soul. Through this, he provides a perspective that goes beyond the immediate context of the war.

The teachings of Krishna, which are found in the Bhagavad Gita, serve as a guiding light that illuminates the path towards achieving spiritual enlightenment. By offering insights into various aspects of life, such as navigating challenges, understanding one's duty, and pursuing spiritual growth, these teachings prove invaluable, especially during times of intense conflicts.

To sum up, the context of the Kurukshetra war in the Mahabharata provides deep understanding into the intricacies of human ethics, the battles fought for fairness and virtue, and the significance of divine intervention in navigating these trials. Lord Krishna's role as a guide and mentor in this epic battle serves as a prime example of the importance of wisdom, compassion, and adherence to dharma when facing the trials and tribulations of life. With its moral and ethical complexities, the war can be seen as a representation of the broader challenges one encounters in life. The lesson it imparts is one of resilience, moral courage, and the necessity of approaching life's challenges with a strong sense of duty and righteousness. The lessons that we can learn from this epic battle, especially the teachings of Krishna, are still relevant and offer valuable guidance and wisdom for dealing with the challenges we encounter in our personal lives.

Resilience in the Face of Adversity

The Kurukshetra war, which is depicted in the epic saga of the Mahabharata, serves as a powerful and profound example of how resilience can be demonstrated in the midst of adversity. In this extensive exploration, we delve deeply into the theme of resilience, examining it through the lens of the epic's characters, with a particular focus on the experiences of the Pandavas and the teachings imparted by Lord Krishna. The essence of resilience is exemplified by the unwavering spirit and steadfastness of these characters, who, guided by Krishna, face numerous challenges and setbacks.

Steadfastness in Turmoil

The Pandavas, who are the central characters in the Mahabharata, serve as a prime example of resilience. Throughout the epic narrative, the protagonists are confronted with a sequence of tests, starting with the unfair punishment of exile and culminating in the devastating moment when they are stripped of their kingdom due to a manipulative game of dice. Throughout their journey, they encounter numerous challenges that serve as tests of their strength, character, and resolve.

Even in the face of these challenges and difficulties, the Pandavas exhibit an unwavering and resilient spirit. Their character is defined by their ability to endure hardship and betrayal with unwavering steadfastness. When we talk about resilience, we are not only talking about physical endurance, but also about mental and spiritual fortitude.

One can clearly observe the remarkable resilience exhibited by the Pandavas throughout the duration of the Kurukshetra war. In the face of the formidable task of reclaiming their rightful kingdom, they bravely confront overwhelming odds with unwavering courage and unyielding determination.

Krishna's Teachings on Resilience

Arjuna, in the midst of the Kurukshetra war, receives profound lessons on resilience from Krishna. Even when faced with overwhelming challenges, he stresses the significance of maintaining both a steady mind and a courageous heart.

The teachings of Krishna highlight the concept that the mind serves as the true battleground. According to him, the key to conquering external challenges lies in advocating for inner strength and fortitude. His teachings highlight the importance of recognizing resilience as a holistic endeavor, encompassing mental, spiritual, and physical aspects.

The Bhagavad Gita, which is a dialogue between Krishna and Arjuna that takes place on the battlefield, is filled with numerous teachings on resilience. Krishna provides guidance to Arjuna, stressing the utmost importance of fulfilling one's duty, staying resolute in one's chosen path, and fostering an unwavering inner resilience that remains undisturbed by external happenings.

The Role of Faith and Determination

The unwavering faith exhibited by the Pandavas further highlights their resilience. Despite the many challenges they have encountered, their belief in dharma (righteousness) and in Krishna's guidance remains unshaken. Their resilience is driven by a crucial element, which is this faith that they hold.

Despite facing multiple setbacks, their unwavering determination to seek justice highlights the strength and resilience of a steadfast mind. The Pandavas' unwavering dedication to reclaiming their kingdom is motivated by their strong sense of duty and commitment to righteousness, highlighting the crucial role that determination plays in fostering resilience.

Lessons in Resilience for Contemporary Times

The lessons that can be learned about resilience from the Kurukshetra war are highly applicable and relevant in today's modern times. In today's world, which is filled with numerous challenges and uncertainties, the importance of resilience, whether on an individual or collective level, is more evident and crucial than ever before.

By examining the teachings of Krishna and observing the example set by the Pandavas, one can gain valuable insights on how to cultivate personal resilience. The evidence presented demonstrates that resilience encompasses the practice of nurturing a calm and composed state of mind, developing emotional strength, and maintaining unwavering determination towards achieving personal objectives.

One of the important aspects covered in the epic is the idea of collective resilience, which can be learned from its lessons. The way in which the Pandavas stood united in the face of adversity serves as a powerful example of how communities and societies can unite and conquer challenges that they face collectively.

Resilience as a Moral and Ethical Strength

The resilience exhibited by the Pandavas goes beyond mere survival; They stand resilient in the face of injustice, symbolizing the importance of upholding righteousness even when it is fraught with challenges.

The portrayal of Krishna as a guide serves as a prime example that highlights the crucial significance of ethical leadership in fostering resilience. One of the main aspects of his teachings is the encouragement for leaders to serve as sources of strength and guidance, thus assisting others in developing resilience during difficult periods.

In closing, the comprehensive analysis presented in "Resilience in the Face of Adversity" delves into the theme of resilience within the context of the Mahabharata, specifically examining its significance in relation to the Kurukshetra war. The narrative of the Pandavas and Krishna's teachings not only entertain but also offer deep insights into the concept of resilience, revealing it to be a powerful amalgamation of inner strength, unwavering faith, relentless determination, and unwavering moral fortitude. The lessons that can be learned from this epic narrative are timeless, as they provide invaluable guidance on how to effectively construct and sustain resilience when confronted with the difficulties that life presents. The teachings of the Mahabharata on resilience continue to hold relevance, whether it be in personal struggles or collective adversities. They offer a comprehensive framework that enables individuals and societies to effectively navigate through obstacles, demonstrating courage, unwavering commitment to righteousness, and steadfastness in their pursuit of overcoming challenges.

Courage and Moral Dilemma

Within the epic narrative of the Mahabharata, there is a thorough exploration of the theme of courage, particularly in relation to moral dilemmas. In this profound exploration, the author delves deep into the intricate nature of courage, examining how it is manifested in the context of upholding Dharma, which encompasses righteousness and duty, amidst the complexities and ethical dilemmas of the Kurukshetra war. Through his dialogues and actions, Krishna serves as a guiding force for the characters, especially Arjuna, as they navigate moral dilemmas and are encouraged to stay committed to the path of righteousness, even when confronted with difficult choices.

Courage in Upholding Dharma

The epic tale of the Mahabharata redefines the concept of true courage. The concept of valor goes beyond the physical bravery displayed in the battlefield and encompasses the moral fortitude required to uphold Dharma. The significance of this type of courage becomes particularly evident in the war, where the battle is not solely focused on territorial gain or political dominance, but rather on the pursuit of righteousness.

One of Krishna's main teachings, as he guides both Arjuna and others, is the crucial role of courage in the preservation of Dharma. One of his main beliefs is the importance of standing firm in the face of moral challenges, and making decisions that prioritize righteousness and justice.

The prime example that encapsulates the essence of this theme is Arjuna's dilemma on the battlefield of Kurukshetra. Arjuna finds himself confronted with the daunting task of engaging in a battle against his own family members, but in this challenging moment, Krishna steps forward as his counselor, offering guidance and leading him on a path of comprehending the profound significance of duty and morality.

Navigating Moral Dilemmas

One of the remarkable aspects of the Mahabharata is its portrayal of a narrative that is abundant with moral complexities and dilemmas. In many instances, characters find themselves confronted with challenging decisions that blur the boundaries between what is considered right and wrong, necessitating a profound exploration of their moral and ethical convictions.

In situations like these, the advice provided by Krishna holds immense importance. Instead of offering simple solutions, he encourages the characters to engage in introspection and gain a deeper understanding of their responsibilities. The purpose of his advice is to assist them in successfully navigating these moral quandaries by encouraging them to embrace a strong sense of ethical responsibility.

In the midst of the war, the characters are confronted with choices that have ethical consequences. The core of Krishna's teachings lies in emphasizing the value of staying committed to one's responsibilities and practicing righteousness, especially when it necessitates great moral courage.

The Confluence of Courage and Ethics

In the narrative of the Mahabharata, there are multiple instances where the characters are required to gather their courage and confront ethical dilemmas. The courage exhibited here extends beyond mere combat against external adversaries; it also involves facing and overcoming inner moral dilemmas.

One of the key elements to take into account in these moral dilemmas is the delicate balance between personal emotions and duty. Many characters in stories find themselves in a constant struggle, torn between their deep affections, complex relationships, and their unwavering commitment to upholding their duty towards Dharma. With the guidance of Krishna, they are able to find a balance, ensuring that their decisions are respectful of both their personal emotions and their ethical obligations.

Courage and Its Manifestations

In the Mahabharata, courage is depicted in both its physical and psychological manifestations. Although warriors exhibit physical bravery during battles, the true measure of their courage is often observed in the mental and ethical challenges they encounter when making morally upright decisions.

The battle against the Kauravas is not merely a quest for power and control over a kingdom, but rather a courageous stance against the prevailing injustice. The Pandavas, under the guidance of Krishna, exhibit tremendous bravery as they bravely confront the injustices committed by the Kauravas, thus serving as a powerful symbol for the fight against all types of wrongdoing.

Krishna's Teachings and Contemporary Relevance

The Mahabharata contains Krishna's teachings, which are filled with enduring wisdom and offer guidance on courage and morality. They emphasize the importance of standing up for what is right, even in the face of daunting challenges.

The relevance of these teachings is profound, especially in the context of contemporary times, where individuals and leaders frequently confront complex ethical dilemmas. Krishna's wise guidance not only helps us navigate through these dilemmas but also provides us with the moral courage and ethical clarity we need.

To conclude, the Mahabharata presents a powerful exploration of the theme of courage when confronted with moral dilemmas, providing deep insights into the complexities of ethical decision-making and the true essence of moral courage. The narrative, which is made more powerful and meaningful by the wisdom of Krishna, emphasizes the significance of upholding righteousness and fulfilling our duties, even in situations that demand great courage and selflessness. The lessons that can be learned from this epic tale are absolutely crucial in order for us to fully comprehend and embrace the concept of courage in our own lives, especially when confronted with difficult ethical dilemmas and intricate moral situations. The teachings of Krishna within the Mahabharata have a profound impact on individuals, serving as a source of inspiration and guiding them to confront the moral dilemmas of life with unwavering courage, profound wisdom, and an unwavering commitment to righteousness.

The Pursuit of Justice

The Kurukshetra war, which is extensively described in the Mahabharata, is a deeply impactful story that centers on the quest for justice within an intricate tapestry of strife, familial connections, and ethical quandaries. The purpose of this comprehensive exploration is to delve into the intricate aspects of this quest for justice. The examination delves into how the war serves as a symbol for the ongoing battle against injustice, as well as the various moral and ethical dilemmas that arise in the process. Lord Krishna, who plays a central role in this narrative, serves as a guide and advocate for justice, making his presence pivotal in the Pandavas' quest. By embarking on this exploration, we delve deep into the intricate layers of Krishna's wisdom and gain a profound understanding of the far-reaching implications of the pursuit of justice in a world riddled with conflict and ethical uncertainty.

Justice Amidst Conflict

The Kurukshetra war goes beyond a mere territorial struggle; it is a profound quest for justice. The representation of the struggle against the forces of injustice is embodied by the unrighteous actions and ambitions of the Kauravas.

The war serves as a prominent example of how seeking justice can be a complex endeavor, especially when the conflict is entangled with familial bonds and long-established relationships. The presence of these complexities adds multiple layers of moral and ethical considerations to the quest for justice.

The reason behind the Pandavas' participation in the war is their relentless pursuit of justice. Their main objective is to regain both their kingdom and the rights that were cunningly snatched away from them. The struggle that they have endured serves as a powerful symbol for the ongoing fight against injustice and the pursuit of restoring righteousness, which is known as Dharma.

Krishna's Role in Seeking Justice

Krishna's involvement in the war surpasses the responsibilities typically associated with a charioteer and advisor. In his emergence, he assumes the position of an advocate of Dharma, providing guidance to the Pandavas as they pursue justice and endeavor to uphold moral values.

Krishna assumes the responsibility of guiding the Pandavas and expertly navigates them through the moral complexities of the war. His counsel not only addresses the immediate scenarios but also ensures the preservation of the larger principles of justice and righteousness.

Krishna's observations throughout the course of the war highlight the concept that the pursuit of justice frequently demands individuals to make tough decisions and engage in challenging actions. Although these decisions may be difficult, they are crucial for the reestablishment and upkeep of ethical harmony within our society.

Moral and Ethical Implications

In the epic tale of the Mahabharata, the characters, particularly the Pandavas, are confronted with the complex task of harmonizing their individual moral principles with the overarching welfare of society. Krishna, with his guidance and wisdom, assists them in successfully navigating this delicate balance, ensuring that their decisions are both ethically sound and in alignment with the pursuit of justice.

Furthermore, the narrative examines the intricate boundary that exists between the search for justice and the longing for vengeance. Krishna's teachings serve the purpose of distinguishing between the two, placing emphasis on the notion that justice should be guided by moral correctness rather than an individual's desire for revenge.

The war, furthermore, brings attention to the sacrifices that are frequently made in the name of justice. The presence of sacrifices, losses, and moral tests along the path to justice is indicative of the challenges one must face.

Krishna's Strategic Wisdom in the Pursuit of Justice

In the Mahabharata, Krishna assumes dual roles, serving not only as a moral guide but also as a strategic mastermind. To ensure that the pursuit of justice is both tactically sound and effective, he employs strategic wisdom.

The strategies implemented by Krishna during the war serve as a testament to the ability to negotiate justice in intricate scenarios, such as warfare. Although his tactics may be controversial at times, his primary objective is to ensure the triumph of Dharma.

Krishna's vision extends beyond the immediate context of the war to include the establishment of a just society. The main focus of his actions and teachings is to construct a societal structure that prioritizes righteousness and justice as its foundation.

The Pursuit of Justice in Contemporary Context

The teachings on justice derived from the Kurukshetra war continue to hold significance in the present era. Within a world that is filled with various injustices and ethical dilemmas, the narrative delves into the principles and obstacles that arise when striving for justice.

The exploration of justice in the Mahabharata serves as a valuable source of lessons for modern legal and societal systems. By emphasizing the importance of moral and ethical considerations, this statement encourages individuals to engage in a thoughtful reflection on how justice is administered and the need for righteousness in judicial processes.

On an individual level, the narrative serves as a source of inspiration for people to advocate for justice in their personal lives. This statement draws attention to the crucial role that righteousness in personal actions plays and emphasizes the responsibility individuals have in upholding justice within their communities.

As a final point, the Mahabharata provides a captivating portrayal of "The Pursuit of Justice" and delves into the intricacies and obstacles encountered in the quest for justice, especially in the context of the Kurukshetra war and the pivotal role played by Krishna. The narrative highlights the significance of maintaining Dharma, making morally responsible choices, and taking strategic factors into account when combating injustice. Krishna's guidance, with its profound wisdom and insightful teachings, acts as a guiding light, helping individuals navigate the complex web of moral dilemmas and ethical quandaries that frequently arise when one is striving for justice. This exploration not only serves the purpose of delving into the intricacies of the ancient epic, but it also has the potential to impart timeless lessons to both contemporary societies and individuals who are actively seeking justice, righteousness, and the establishment of a more equitable world.

Lessons in Leadership and Strategy from the Kurukshetra War

The Kurukshetra war, as portrayed in the Mahabharata, serves as an intricate and significant arena where not only moral and ethical principles clash, but also where valuable insights into leadership and strategy can be derived. The purpose of this extensive exploration is to delve into the strategic insights that can be derived from the war, with a specific emphasis on the role of Krishna as a guide and strategist. The book explores how Krishna's extensive knowledge of warfare, diplomacy, and human psychology shapes his strategic choices and leadership approach, and demonstrates how these valuable insights can be applied to effectively navigate intricate and difficult circumstances.

Strategic Insights from the War

One can witness Krishna's unparalleled strategic brilliance in action through the Kurukshetra war, which serves as a prime example of his abilities. His guidance extends beyond mere physical warfare and encompasses a comprehensive understanding of strategy, diplomacy, and psychological warfare, which he shares with the Pandavas.

Krishna's strategy in the war is holistic, meaning it considers all factors and elements. His considerations encompass a wide range of factors, including but not limited to the morale of the warriors, the tactical formations employed in battle, the psychological tactics employed, as well as the larger ethical implications of engaging in warfare.

Krishna's involvement in the diplomatic negotiations that preceded the war, as well as his dedicated efforts to avert the war through peaceful methods, serve as a testament to his remarkable diplomatic skills and astute understanding of the intricacies of diplomacy. His approach to strategizing incorporates a thoughtful mix of foresight, effective negotiation techniques, and a firm adherence to ethical standards.

Leading in Complex Situations

Krishna's leadership during the war is characterized by his remarkable skill in navigating intricate situations with wisdom and foresight, which is one of the key aspects that sets him apart. Recognizing the complexity of the conflict, he provides astute counsel to the Pandavas, guiding them through its intricacies.

One notable aspect of Krishna's leadership style is the way he skillfully balances ethical considerations with tactical necessity. While he understands the significance of upholding Dharma (the moral and ethical code), he also acknowledges the practicalities of warfare.

Krishna's interactions with different characters clearly demonstrate his high level of emotional intelligence. Utilizing his comprehensive understanding of their motivations, fears, and strengths, he effectively guides, motivates, and at times, soothes them.

Krishna's Tactical Brilliance

Krishna, throughout the Kurukshetra war, demonstrates his brilliance by devising innovative strategies and formations. His contributions to the formulation of battle tactics, such as the Chakravyuha, as well as his implementation of unconventional methods, serve as evidence of his exceptional tactical brilliance.

Krishna incorporates psychological strategies into his methods as well. One aspect of his strategies is that they frequently involve tactics that aim to demoralize the enemy or generate confusion and doubt, which demonstrates his grasp of the psychological aspects of warfare.

Krishna's strategic leadership stands out due to his remarkable ability to adapt to different situations. When faced with changing dynamics on the battlefield, he demonstrates an impressive ability to quickly respond and adapt his strategies in real-time, all in an effort to gain a strategic advantage.

Ethical Dilemmas and Decision Making

Given the numerous ethical dilemmas arising from the war, Krishna's role in addressing and resolving them is absolutely crucial. In his role, he assists the Pandavas in making tough choices that not only demonstrate tactical wisdom but also align with the principles of righteousness.

One way to analyze Krishna's strategies and decisions is by examining them in the context of the Just War theory. He strongly advocates for engaging in the war in a manner that is both just and moral, ensuring the principles of righteous warfare are upheld.

Krishna's Teachings and Modern Leadership

The strategic insights and leadership lessons that can be derived from Krishna's role in the Kurukshetra war hold immense relevance and applicability in today's leadership scenarios. When considering his blend of strategic acumen, ethical considerations, and emotional intelligence, it becomes clear that he offers a comprehensive model for effective leadership in complex situations.

Krishna's strategies offer invaluable insights and teachings for individuals engaging in strategic thinking across various fields such as business, politics, and other domains. The relevance of his skills, such as his ability to anticipate challenges, understand stakeholder motivations, and navigate through complex situations, is particularly important for leaders in the modern world.

The leadership displayed by Krishna during the war serves as a powerful reminder of the significance of ethics and moral responsibility. The approach he adopts in today's context underscores the importance for leaders to prioritize decisions that are both strategically sound and ethically righteous.

To conclude, the Kurukshetra war, as depicted in the Mahabharata, provides valuable insights into leadership and strategy, with a special focus on the pivotal role of Krishna. When you combine his strategic insights, ethical considerations, and emotional intelligence, you get a comprehensive guide that can help you lead effectively in complex situations. Krishna's exceptional leadership throughout the duration of the war serves as a prime example of how one can seamlessly integrate strategic brilliance, ethical decision-making, and emotional understanding. The lessons derived from the epic narrative hold immense value for leaders in the present day, providing them with valuable insights on how to effectively navigate the intricate challenges of modern leadership while maintaining a sense of balance and ethical conduct.

Embracing Life's Challenges

Life as a Battlefield

The Mahabharata presents life as a battleground, a figurative setting where individuals confront a multitude of trials and tribulations. The challenges that individuals face can vary greatly, encompassing personal dilemmas, internal conflicts, external adversities, and societal pressures.

By showcasing this portrayal, it becomes evident that the struggle in life is something that persists without interruption. In the same way that the warriors in the Mahabharata are confronted with relentless challenges during their battles, people in life experience ongoing trials that put their strength, resilience, and character to the test.

According to the teachings of the epic, adversities should not be seen merely as obstacles, but rather as valuable opportunities for personal growth and self-discovery. With every challenge that comes our way, we are presented with an opportunity to learn, grow, and come out even stronger.

Balancing Duties and Ethics

The concept of Dharma, which refers to the righteous duty, is a central theme that is explored in the Mahabharata. Krishna's teachings place great importance on the idea of fulfilling one's obligations and responsibilities in life, all the while remaining dedicated to upholding moral and ethical values.

The epic demonstrates that in life, there are often situations that arise where one's duties and ethical principles may appear to be in conflict with each other. Krishna's guidance plays a crucial role in helping individuals navigate the intricate complexities of life, ensuring that their actions are in accordance with their personal responsibilities as well as ethical standards.

In the epic, the journey of the Pandavas serves as a prime example of the constant struggle to find a balance between fulfilling one's duties and upholding ethical principles. Krishna's guidance plays a significant role in shaping their decisions, which are made with the intention of upholding this balance, particularly in the face of challenging situations.

Spiritual Insights in Difficult Times

The Bhagavad Gita, which is a sacred conversation between Krishna and Arjuna, contains a multitude of profound spiritual teachings that hold special significance during challenging periods. By engaging with these teachings, individuals can gain a more profound comprehension of the fundamental aspects of life, including its nature, the obligations that come with it, and the transient nature of earthly tribulations.

According to Krishna's teachings, although life's challenges may appear overwhelming, they are temporary in nature. The key to truly experiencing the essence of existence is to grasp the impermanence of these challenges and dedicate oneself to spiritual growth and self-realization.

One can find valuable guidance in the Gita when it comes to attaining inner peace and developing resilience. The main idea behind it is to encourage people to detach themselves from materialistic aspects and instead concentrate on developing their inner spirituality, which in turn equips them with the ability to face life's challenges with a composed and unwavering mindset.

The Role of Faith and Understanding

One of the central themes in Krishna's teachings is the importance of placing faith in the divine plan. One of his core beliefs is that individuals should have faith in the idea that every challenge they face serves a purpose in the grand cosmic scheme, and that every adversity they encounter is actually a necessary step towards their spiritual evolution.

One of the key elements in Krishna's teachings revolves around the concept of recognizing and comprehending the true essence of oneself, referred to as the soul, which is eternal and transcends the temporary challenges encountered in life. Having this understanding greatly aids in confronting life's challenges with a sense of detachment and clarity.

Life Lessons from the Mahabharata

The characters presented in the Mahabharata, with their wide range of personalities and complex dilemmas, serve as a source of invaluable life lessons. The stories they tell serve as a powerful lesson on various aspects such as strength, weakness, virtue, vice, and the intricate dynamics of human emotions and choices.

The lessons that can be learned from the Mahabharata hold a great deal of relevance in today's contemporary society. One of the benefits of their guidance is that they offer valuable insights on how to navigate both personal and professional challenges. Additionally, they provide guidance on making ethical decisions and finding spiritual meaning along life's journey.

To sum up, the Mahabharata, with its theme of "Embracing Life's Challenges," especially through the teachings of Krishna, provides a complete roadmap for successfully maneuvering through the challenges that life throws at us. The epic serves as a framework through which one can gain a deeper understanding of life's adversities, learn how to balance duties with ethics, and acquire valuable spiritual insights during challenging moments. The wisdom imparted by Krishna in the Bhagavad Gita serves as a beacon of guidance, providing valuable perspectives that assist individuals in overcoming the trials and tribulations of the material world while redirecting their focus towards attaining elevated spiritual objectives. In the Mahabharata, life is metaphorically portrayed as a battlefield, emphasizing the need for individuals to persistently combat internal and external challenges. This metaphor is a powerful inspiration, urging people to navigate life's obstacles with resilience, ethical clarity, and spiritual wisdom.

Conclusion: Learning from the Battlefield of Life

The Kurukshetra war, which is a significant event in the Mahabharata, goes beyond its historical or mythological background. It serves as a symbol of the timeless battle between what is right and what is wrong, and the complex moral and ethical challenges that humans encounter. In many ways, this war acts as a small-scale version of the larger battles we encounter in life, where individuals are always grappling with obstacles that originate from both external sources and their own inner struggles.

Timeless Lessons from Krishna

One of the key lessons that Krishna imparts in the Mahabharata is the significance of cultivating resilience when confronted with challenging circumstances. By guiding the Pandavas, he effectively demonstrates that resilience is not solely about enduring hardships but also about confronting them with both strength and wisdom.

The courage exhibited during the Kurukshetra war transcends mere physical bravery. The act embodies a great deal of moral courage as it involves upholding one's righteous duty, known as Dharma, even when faced with immense challenges. In his dialogues, Krishna, especially in the Bhagavad Gita, puts great emphasis on the significance of taking a stand for what is morally and ethically correct.

The role that Krishna plays in the war serves as a prime example of how justice can be a complex and multifaceted concept. With his advocacy, he guides the Pandavas in their rightful quest against injustice and moral corruption, advocating for a justice that is tempered with wisdom and compassion.

Embracing Life's Challenges

Symbolically representing life as a battlefield, the Mahabharata illustrates the multitude of challenges that individuals encounter, which serve as a means to assess their character, beliefs, and resilience. In times of difficulty, Krishna's teachings provide a valuable framework that encourages individuals to navigate challenges, emphasizing the importance of maintaining a balance between fulfilling one's duty and upholding personal ethics, while also emphasizing the pursuit of spiritual insight.

The war has taught us a valuable lesson about the delicate equilibrium between meeting one's responsibilities and staying true to ethical standards. Krishna's guidance to not only Arjuna but also other characters serves to shed light on the path of righteous action, even when faced with the most intricate and challenging circumstances.

The teachings and spiritual wisdom shared by Krishna, specifically in the Bhagavad Gita, carry great significance and are of profound importance. Their guidance provides insight into how to comprehend the temporary nature of life's challenges while emphasizing the timeless principles of duty, righteousness, and the spiritual voyage of the soul.

Krishna's Wisdom as a Guiding Light

The teachings of Krishna, with a particular emphasis on his strategic and ethical insights, remain highly relevant and applicable throughout different time periods. The guidance they offer is specifically tailored for individuals and leaders in today's world, helping them navigate the intricate challenges and moral quandaries of modern life.

With a wide range of personalities and experiences, the characters in the Mahabharata contribute to a tapestry of lessons that are incredibly rich and diverse. The journeys of these individuals, which have been greatly influenced by Krishna's wisdom, offer valuable insights into the complexities of human nature, the profound consequences of our choices, and the transformative paths towards redemption and self-realization.

The teachings of Krishna in the Mahabharata serve as a valuable guide, offering insights not just for personal growth and spiritual enlightenment but also for the development of society as a whole. The encouragement of cultivating qualities like resilience, courage, justice, and moral integrity is highly emphasized as they are crucial for the advancement and betterment of societies.

In summary, the essence of "Battlefield Illumination: Embracing Life's Challenges" lies in its ability to encapsulate the profound insights gained from the Kurukshetra war, emphasizing the essential role played by resilience, courage, and the pursuit of justice in navigating the various obstacles that life presents. At its core, The Mahabharata is a metaphorical guide for life, infused with Krishna's wisdom, providing valuable insights on how to handle challenges, make ethical decisions, and effectively lead during turbulent phases. The epic's narrative is not only rich in wisdom and moral insights but also serves as a powerful encouragement for individuals to tackle life's challenges with strength, wisdom, and integrity. Serving as a guiding beacon, it helps us navigate the intricacies of life by combining a balanced approach that harmonizes duty and ethics, as well as worldly responsibilities and spiritual development.

Chapter Nine

Chapter 9: Miracle of the Mountain

Faith and the Power of Protection

The Story of Govardhan Hill

In Vrindavan, the story of Krishna's enchanting childhood begins. The inhabitants of this lush, pastoral town were steeped in tradition, one of which was performing an elaborate sacrifice to Indra, the god of rain, crucial for their agricultural lifestyle.

The villagers considered the annual sacrifice to be a momentous occasion, as they believed it played a crucial role in bringing timely rains and bountiful harvests. With an overwhelming sense of fervor, the community made extensive preparations for this event, highlighting their deep faith and reliance on divine forces for their sustenance.

Witnessing the extensive preparations, Young Krishna's curiosity is piqued and he begins to question the purpose of these elaborate rituals. By asking thought-provoking questions, he manages to awaken a sense of inquiry among the villagers, challenging their unquestioning adherence to tradition without grasping its underlying essence.

Krishna, using his persuasive and insightful words, motivates and encourages the villagers to show reverence and respect towards Govardhan Hill. According to his argument, the hill, which is rich in forests, rivers, and fertile lands, serves as a direct source of their necessities, making it deserving of their reverence.

The change in emphasis from worshiping gods to valuing and honoring the natural world demonstrates a profound regard for the environment. Krishna's message brings attention to the crucial role of acknowledging and valuing the natural resources that are essential for sustaining life.

Indra, the god of rain, is angered by the villagers' shift in devotion, leading him to decide on punishing them as a form of retribution. The wrathful force of his fury is unleashed upon the humble town of Vrindavan, causing a monstrous storm that not only puts the lives of its inhabitants at risk but also endangers the well-being of their beloved livestock.

The storm, which is being described as unprecedented, is causing widespread devastation due to its torrential rains and fierce winds. Overwhelmed by fear and a feeling of helplessness, the villagers instinctively look to Krishna as their savior.

Witnessing their suffering, Krishna feels compelled to intervene and performs a miracle that can only be attributed to his divine power. With his little finger, he effortlessly raises the entire Govardhan Hill, creating a protective shelter for the entire village. The miraculous act performed by Krishna serves a dual purpose - it not only shields the villagers from the storm but also strengthens their belief in his divine nature.

Lessons from the Govardhan Episode

The act of lifting Govardhan Hill serves as a powerful metaphor, illustrating the supremacy of genuine faith in contrast to superficial ritualistic practices. The act performed by Krishna serves as a lesson, highlighting the importance of sincere devotion and gratitude towards nature and its resources, emphasizing that these aspects hold greater significance than mere blind ritualistic offerings.

The main focus of this episode is to showcase the theme of divine compassion and how it serves as a source of protection for devoted individuals. Krishna's intervention serves as a powerful illustration that the divine is forever responsive and attentive to the genuine prayers and requirements of those who have unwavering faith.

Another valuable takeaway from the story is the importance of maintaining a harmonious relationship with nature. Krishna emphasizes the importance of honoring Govardhan Hill as a means to promote a sustainable relationship with the environment, advocating for the respect and protection of its natural bounty.

The story of Govardhan Hill is not only culturally significant but also holds immense spiritual value. The festival of Govardhan Puja is celebrated annually as a reminder to people about the significance of faith, gratitude, and respect for nature.

The story continues to resonate with themes of environmental conservation and the urgent need for us to reevaluate our connection with nature in today's world. This serves as a powerful reminder for us to cherish and protect the natural world, which is responsible for sustaining all forms of life.

Along with its entertainment value, the episode delves into the subject of spiritual growth and the significance of devotion. This approach fosters an intimate and direct connection with the divine, going beyond traditional rituals and prioritizing authentic devotion and heartfelt gratitude.

In summary, the account of Govardhan Hill weaves together themes of faith, divine intervention, and a strong commitment to environmental consciousness. The story beautifully illustrates the way in which a young Krishna, with his profound wisdom and divine powers, leads his devotees on a journey towards a deeper understanding of faith, a greater respect for nature, and an appreciation for the power of divine protection. The narrative from the Mahabharata, despite its mythological origins, transcends its context to deliver invaluable lessons that hold immense relevance in our modern society. Encouragement is found in the act of cultivating a sincere devotion, living in harmony with nature, and trusting in the divine protection that guards us against life's adversities. Therefore, the story of Govardhan Hill not only provides spiritual inspiration but also offers valuable guidance on how to live a life that is infused with faith, gratitude, and a profound appreciation for the beauty of nature.

Symbolism of the Govardhan Episode

The episode of Govardhan holds great importance as it signifies a notable transition from mere ritualistic practices to sincere and genuine faith. Krishna encourages a shift away from traditional methods of appeasing gods through sacrifices, advocating for a more heartfelt and authentic form of devotion.

The actions of Krishna serve as a powerful symbol of liberation from the constraints of ritualistic worship. Through his actions, he shows that genuine devotion is not defined by extravagant ceremonies but rather by a deep belief in and comprehension of the divine.

The main message conveyed in this episode is that regular individuals have the power to empower themselves, as it demonstrates that connecting with the divine does not necessitate intermediaries or complex rituals, but can instead be attained through sincere and uncomplicated devotion.

The act performed by Krishna, where he lifted Govardhan Hill, serves as a powerful symbol that represents the availability of divine protection for individuals who possess unwavering faith. By directly demonstrating how belief in the divine can serve as a safe haven during difficult times, this act highlights the power of faith.

The episode serves as a powerful illustration, demonstrating how faith can function as a protective shield in the face of adversities. The faith that the villagers have in Krishna's divinity and power acts as a shield against Indra's fury, demonstrating how faith has the ability to conquer even the most daunting obstacles.

The symbolic significance of the protection Krishna offers to the inhabitants of Vrindavan lies in its parallel to the spiritual salvation that faith can provide. The metaphor signifies that by sincerely devoting oneself and placing trust in the divine, one can attain divine grace.

Krishna's encouragement of the villagers to honor Govardhan Hill leads to a shift in focus, moving from deity worship to the importance of respecting and valuing natural resources. The act of acknowledging the gifts of nature is symbolized by this action, highlighting its importance.

One of the key takeaways from the Govardhan episode is the significance of promoting environmental consciousness. This teaches us the importance of showing respect and protection towards nature, in all its various forms, as it is indispensable for the continuation of life.

The teachings presented by Krishna in this episode shed light on how closely humans are intertwined with the world around them. The forefront of our minds is where the idea that the well-being of humanity is intricately tied to the health and sanctity of the natural world is emphasized.

In this episode, one of the key teachings is the significance of showing humility when confronted with the overwhelming and mighty forces of nature. It is important to remember that even with all our progress and abilities, humans are still subject to the power of nature.

The act of worshiping Govardhan Hill is a way for individuals to show their appreciation for the abundance that nature offers. The main purpose of this is to instill a feeling of thankfulness and appreciation towards the resources that are essential for human survival.

By acting in a way that goes against the established religious and societal norms, Krishna challenges their validity. The act of questioning the need for elaborate sacrifices to Indra results in a transformation in the way divine worship and nature are understood.

As a result of the events in the episode, there is a noticeable shift in the collective consciousness of the villagers. They transition away from a fear-based form of worship, which is centered around rituals, and adopt a more conscious and enlightened approach that emphasizes devotion and respect for nature.

The teachings and insights gained from the Govardhan episode remain highly pertinent in the present day. In today's society, where the degradation of the environment is a pressing concern, this story serves as a powerful reminder of the urgent need for environmental stewardship and the importance of respecting our natural resources.

In today's world, the theme of faith over rituals is particularly relevant, as spiritual practices can easily transform into mere rituals lacking genuine devotion. By examining Krishna's teachings, individuals are invited to re-evaluate their personal faith and devotion, which can lead to a more sincere and purposeful spiritual practice.

The main objective of the episode is to promote a harmonious vision that encompasses both spirituality and the environment. The suggestion is that when it comes to spiritual growth and environmental consciousness, they can work together harmoniously, resulting in a more well-rounded and sustainable way of living.

To conclude, it is worth mentioning that the Govardhan episode is not only a captivating story but also a rich source of symbolism and profound teachings. This statement emphasizes three key themes: the superiority of faith over mere ritualistic worship, the strength derived from divine protection, and the significance of showing reverence and safeguarding the environment. In this episode, Krishna imparts teachings that transcend time and offer wisdom that is relevant even today. These teachings inspire a transformation from mere ritualistic devotion to a more sincere and heartfelt faith. Additionally, they encourage environmental consciousness, urging us to be more mindful of our impact on the planet. Moreover, Krishna's teachings promote a deeper connection with the divine, allowing us to experience a profound spiritual bond. With its abundance of spiritual and ecological insights, this story serves as a guiding light, illuminating the path towards embracing a life filled with faith, humility, gratitude, and a deep sense of harmony with nature. The narrative's power lies in its ability to deeply resonate with the spiritual and environmental challenges faced in the modern world, thereby serving as an inspiration for adopting a balanced approach to spirituality and environmental stewardship.

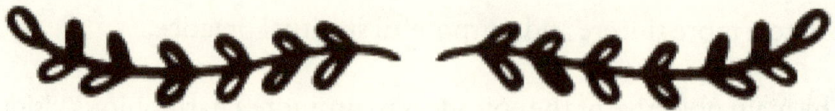

Lessons in Faith and Devotion from the Govardhan Episode

The villagers of Vrindavan, in the face of the devastating storm caused by Indra, demonstrate their unwavering faith in Krishna. Despite the dire situation, their faith remains unwavering, serving as a powerful symbol of the strength and unwavering dedication that comes with unconditional devotion.

The villagers' faith begins to revolve around Krishna, who, at that time, is a young boy. The deep trust in Krishna's divine power, even though he appears youthful, highlights the core of genuine faith that transcends the physical and logical aspects.

The faith that the villagers have in Krishna goes beyond what can be explained by reason and logic. The unwavering faith in question is one that remains steadfast even in the face of seemingly insurmountable odds, demonstrating that true devotion does not rely on comprehension or justification.

The reason why Krishna lifted Govardhan Hill was because he wanted to directly respond to the immense devotion shown by the villagers. By demonstrating unwavering faith, this act symbolizes the divine's reciprocation and serves as a testament to the notion that sincere devotion is always acknowledged by the divine.

Symbolically, Govardhan Hill represents the protective embrace that shields devotees, extending its grace to the villagers who find refuge under its watchful presence. Krishna's answer serves as a prime example, showcasing the constant willingness of the divine to safeguard and provide for those who entrust themselves to it.

The miraculous act performed by Krishna not only showcases his power, but also emphasizes the intricate relationship between human faith and divine will. The fact is, when it comes to faith, the devotee offers it willingly, but in return, they receive the gifts of divine protection and reciprocation.

One of the lessons conveyed by the episode is the idea that having faith can act as a strong protective barrier against the challenges and hardships that life throws our way. The villagers' sheltered state under the protective cover of Govardhan Hill serves as a symbol of how faith can serve as a sanctuary and offer a sense of safety during turbulent times.

Furthermore, the story highlights the notion that facing challenges and adversities can actually deepen and solidify one's faith. The experience of enduring the storm and receiving Krishna's protection further solidifies the faith of the villagers, making it both stronger and more profound.

Resilience is a key theme highlighted in the Govardhan episode, making it a valuable source of lessons. This illustrates that having faith instills a special resilience in people, allowing them to not only face challenges head-on but also triumph over them with a positive mindset.

The Govardhan episode offers valuable lessons of faith and devotion that are still relevant and hold great significance in today's world. The episode serves as a poignant reminder of the role and significance of faith in human existence, particularly in a world where skepticism and rationality often hold sway.

The Govardhan episode is remarkable not only for its significance but also for the communal aspect of faith it portrays. By coming together and sharing their faith, the villagers have formed a unified force that showcases the strength of shared belief and communal support when confronted with collective obstacles.

Furthermore, the episode not only entertains but also educates viewers about the importance of having faith in the environment and treating it with respect. The fact that the villagers hold Govardhan Hill in such high regard, recognizing its role as a provider of resources, serves as a powerful reminder of the imperative to coexist harmoniously with nature, demonstrating respect and gratitude.

To sum up, the "Lessons in Faith and Devotion" derived from the Govardhan episode in the Mahabharata provides deep and meaningful understandings regarding the interplay between faith and the reciprocation of the divine. The idea conveyed here is that having complete trust in a spiritual force can lead to extraordinary accomplishments, both in the literal sense of moving mountains and in a metaphorical sense as well. The emphasis placed by Krishna on the divine's responsiveness to faith underscores the idea that true devotion is always met with divine protection and grace. The main lesson conveyed by this narrative is that faith is more than just a belief; it is a formidable force that has the ability to conquer even the most difficult obstacles in life. By encouraging a reinvigoration of faith and devotion in modern life, it serves as a reminder of their enduring significance, providing strength, protection, and resilience. The story of Govardhan Hill serves as a lesson that transcends time, teaching us about the immense power of faith and the unwavering protection bestowed upon us by the divine, ultimately motivating individuals to wholeheartedly adopt faith as a guiding principle in their lives.

Integrating the Govardhan Lesson into Life

The Govardhan episode serves as a timeless reminder of the power and relevance of faith, especially in an era characterized by rapid change and uncertainty. This example perfectly illustrates the power of faith to offer comfort and resilience, particularly during times of hardship.

The episode emphasizes the importance of individuals fostering a strong inner belief in order to achieve their goals. In the fast-paced world that we live in today, where materialism is often prioritized, having such inner strength can provide a sense of comfort and resilience.

Similar to how the villagers' unwavering faith in Krishna served as a safeguard, having faith in modern life can serve as a protective shield, providing individuals with the mental and emotional strength needed to overcome life's trials and tribulations.

Another aspect that the story brings attention to is the necessity of maintaining a harmonious equilibrium between rationality and faith. In today's modern era where scientific thought and skepticism prevail, the Govardhan episode serves as a powerful reminder that faith continues to hold a significant place in the lives of humanity.

Demonstrating honor towards Govardhan Hill highlights the imperative of valuing and safeguarding the natural world. A key takeaway from this is that faith should extend beyond individual beliefs and encompass a sense of responsibility towards the environment.

According to the episode, true devotion encompasses more than just personal salvation; it also entails taking responsibility for the world around us. A balanced approach is necessary in which faith and practical actions work together to benefit both nature and society.

The story of Govardhan has the potential to inspire sustainable living practices that not only honor and protect the environment but also show that spirituality and environmental consciousness can coexist in perfect harmony.

The teachings of Krishna during the Govardhan episode are filled with profound spiritual wisdom. They encourage individuals to reflect on the essence of devotion, highlighting the importance of understanding that true devotion encompasses more than mere ritualistic practices.

The story acts as a catalyst, sparking personal growth and development. This encourages individuals to delve deep into the depths of their faith, allowing them to gain a profound understanding of themselves and the world around them.

The Govardhan episode provides valuable insights that shed light on the intricate dynamics between humans and the divine. The illustration clearly shows that the relationship between humans and the divine is dynamic and reciprocal, with sincere human devotion being met with divine compassion and protection.

The story serves as an excellent example of how faith can possess a particularly potent strength during moments of hardship. When faced with immense challenges, it becomes evident that faith can serve as a guiding light, offering both hope and guidance.

Witnessing the incredible resilience displayed by the villagers under Govardhan Hill has the potential to inspire individuals to cultivate a comparable level of resilience in their own lives, relying on faith as a fundamental pillar to overcome and conquer personal challenges.

By acknowledging and showing gratitude for the small 'mountains' that support and safeguard us, we can incorporate the teachings of Govardhan into our daily lives. One way to interpret this is by expressing gratitude for the blessings we have received in life and by showing respect towards the natural world.

Another key aspect emphasized in the episode is the significance of community and how it can be strengthened through shared beliefs and faith. The encouragement lies in the development of communities where faith is not only shared but also nurtured, ultimately resulting in the growth of collective strength and unity.

Within a diverse and pluralistic world, the Govardhan episode provides an opportunity for faith to be reinterpreted in a manner that is inclusive and adaptable to the various contexts of modern society.

Consequently, this encourages a universal understanding of spiritual principles.

To summarize, when we incorporate the teachings from the Govardhan episode into our lives, we are presented with an opportunity to develop a strong inner faith, maintain a harmonious relationship with nature and society, and gain valuable spiritual knowledge that can greatly impact our personal development. The story of Krishna's feat of lifting Govardhan Hill extends beyond its mythical origins to offer meaningful and practical insights for today's society. One of the main objectives of this initiative is to encourage individuals to view faith as not only a source of strength and protection but also as a guiding force for their actions towards the environment and a catalyst for embarking on a more profound exploration of their spiritual journey. By extension, the Govardhan episode takes on a significance that goes beyond its portrayal as a mythological narrative.

Conclusion: Embracing the Miracle of Faith

The Govardhan episode holds much more significance than a mere mythological tale. The act of Krishna lifting Govardhan Hill is not just a historical event, but also a symbolic representation that holds significance across different time periods and cultures. It teaches us valuable lessons about faith, the intervention of the divine, and the significance of living in harmony with nature.

The story serves as an example of how one can maintain unwavering faith in the power of the divine. In Vrindavan, the villagers, who have complete trust in Krishna, are fortunate enough to witness a miraculous event that rescues them from a disastrous storm. By demonstrating this act of faith, we are showcasing the undeniable power and protective qualities that faith can bring into our lives.

The episode of Govardhan serves as a powerful example to demonstrate how divine forces show responsiveness to the faith and devotion of human beings. By lifting the hill, Krishna directly responded to the faith of the villagers, emphasizing that pure and unwavering faith invites divine protection and intervention.

Through its storytelling, the narrative imparts the valuable lesson that having faith can provide individuals with a strong and impenetrable shield, enabling them to face and overcome the adversities of life. Similar to how the villagers found shelter and protection under the Govardhan Hill, faith has the ability to create a protective canopy during life's difficult storms.

The episode of Govardhan serves as a significant reminder of the importance of coexisting harmoniously with the natural world. The villagers demonstrate a profound respect for nature by honoring the hill, which in turn reciprocates by providing them with essential resources and protecting their environment.

Furthermore, the story highlights the correlation between environmental stewardship and spirituality. The suggestion is that genuine spirituality involves not only a profound reverence for the environment but also actively promoting sustainable and harmonious ways of living.

The lessons that can be learned from the Govardhan episode hold great significance even in today's modern era. In today's society, characterized by environmental crises and a pervasive lack of faith, this story serves as a powerful reminder of the significance of nurturing faith and embracing a harmonious coexistence with nature.

The story not only encourages individuals to cultivate faith in personal challenges but also emphasizes the importance of addressing collective societal issues. The main point emphasized here is that when faith is combined with collective action, it has the power to bring about meaningful and impactful transformations.

Apart from its main purpose, the Govardhan episode also plays a pivotal role in fostering personal spiritual growth. By encouraging introspection and fostering a deeper understanding of one's relationship with the divine, it paves the way for a transformative journey towards spiritual enlightenment.

The narrative of Govardhan serves as an inspiration for a life that is guided by faith. According to the suggestion, embracing faith has the potential to result in a life that is more fulfilled, protected, and spiritually enriched.

Another important message conveyed in the story is the importance of maintaining a harmonious equilibrium between faith and practical obligations, particularly in relation to environmental stewardship. To truly embrace life, one must adopt an approach that merges spiritual faith with responsible actions towards the natural world.

Throughout the episode, viewers are reminded of the remarkable impact that collective faith and a spirit of community can have. The demonstration of a community uniting in faith and harmony with nature showcases its ability to conquer significant obstacles and prosper.

In summary, "Miracle of the Mountain: Faith and the Power of Protection" serves as a comprehensive representation of the profound teachings found within the Govardhan episode. The metaphorical guide serves multiple purposes, encouraging individuals to embrace faith and devotion in their lives, fostering a harmonious relationship with the environment, and finding strength and protection in the divine. This narrative, which is filled with both spiritual and ecological wisdom, serves as a guiding light, offering hope and direction, and encouraging individuals to develop a deeper comprehension of the significance of faith when it comes to overcoming life's obstacles and fostering a profound bond with the divine. The episode of Govardhan, with its teachings that stand the test of time, continues to be a compelling narrative for individuals in search of spiritual development, awareness of the environment, and a life centered on faith and harmony.

Chapter Ten

Chapter 10: Ras Leela:

The Dance of Cosmic Love

The Mystical Dance of Ras Leela

The Ras Leela, a divine dance drama, takes place in the enchanting town of Vrindavan, which is renowned for being the backdrop of Krishna's remarkable adventures, particularly on moonlit nights. The night's celestial ambiance provides the perfect backdrop, creating an atmosphere that elevates this event from the ordinary to the extraordinary, immersing participants in a realm that is truly divine.

With utmost grace, Krishna, known as the divine incarnation, extends a warm invitation to the Gopis, inviting them to partake in his presence. We extend this invitation not only for you to join us in a dance, but also for you to embark on a sacred journey that represents the soul's quest for ultimate enlightenment and oneness with the divine.

With eager anticipation and overwhelming ecstasy, the Gopis come together, irresistibly drawn by the captivating sound of Krishna's flute. The immediate response shown by individuals to Krishna's call is a reflection of the deep longing within the soul to unite with the divine, surpassing any worldly attachments.

The Ras Leela, a traditional dance performance, symbolizes the perpetual dance of the universe and its eternal rhythm. In this beautiful and profound concept, known as divine play or Leela, Krishna, who represents the supreme consciousness, partakes in a mesmerizing dance of cosmic love and joy with the Gopis, who symbolize individual souls.

Through the dance, the divine essence of Krishna merges harmoniously with the individual souls of the Gopis, symbolizing the ultimate union. The concept symbolizes the progression of the soul's spiritual expedition, moving from the constraints of the ego to the limitless expanse of divine love and consciousness.

Through its circular formation, the Ras Leela dance effectively embodies the intricate interplay between life, death, and rebirth, serving as a poignant metaphor for the soul's transformative journey towards achieving complete oneness with the divine. The circle, much like the eternal nature of the soul, symbolizes the universe's infinite existence without any boundaries or limitations.

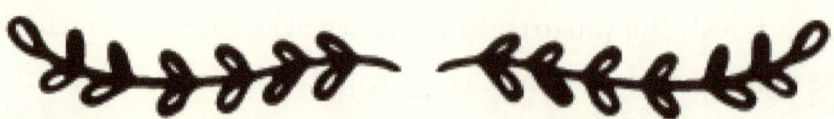

The call of Krishna's flute, which has the power to lure the Gopis to the dance, represents the divine call that awakens the soul and guides it towards its true purpose. It represents the spiritual awakening that beckons the soul towards a higher consciousness.

By forsaking their worldly duties and joining Krishna's dance, the Gopis symbolize the profound journey of the soul, as it strives to transcend the illusions and attachments of the material realm, in its relentless pursuit of divine love and ultimate truth.

During the Ras Leela, an enchanting performance, Krishna mysteriously manifests himself to dance with every Gopi at the same time, which serves as a profound representation of the inherent unity that exists in all beings. The illustration highlights the idea that even though individual souls may seem distinct, they are ultimately interconnected as integral components of the supreme consciousness.

With its profound symbolism, the Ras Leela serves as a representation of the path of Bhakti in Hindu philosophy. By showcasing pure devotion, love, and surrender, it becomes evident that the soul can experience divine bliss and unite with the supreme consciousness.

The dance not only provides a captivating performance, but it also symbolizes the profound process of discovering oneself. The key aspect that is being highlighted here is the progression of the soul's journey, starting from a place of ignorance and gradually moving towards enlightenment, with Krishna serving as the guiding force.

Various spiritual traditions have offered their own interpretations of the Ras Leela, a dance that holds deep spiritual significance, each offering a unique perspective on its symbolism. Some interpretations of it perceive it as a metaphor representing the dynamic relationship between the material and spiritual dimensions, whereas other viewpoints regard it as an allegory symbolizing the liberation of the soul from the perpetual cycle of life and death.

Countless artistic expressions have been influenced by the Ras Leela, encompassing classical dance, music, painting, and literature. The rich symbolism and profound spiritual messages depicted in these art forms have made the Ras Leela an enduring theme in Indian culture.

Festivals in regions closely linked to Krishna's life are known for their vibrant celebrations of the Ras Leela, a dance-drama that showcases Krishna's divine love. The celebrations that take place are not solely cultural events, but rather they hold a profound spiritual meaning. They offer devotees a chance to immerse themselves in the divine love and joy that the Ras Leela represents.

To conclude, "The Mystical Dance of Ras Leela" provides a profound exploration of one of the most enigmatic and spiritually enriching events in Hindu mythology, leaving audiences captivated and enlightened. The Ras Leela goes beyond being just a dance; it transforms into a powerful symbol that represents the eternal play of the universe, the delightful and affectionate exchange between the divine and the individual soul, and the ultimate union of spirituality. Serving as a metaphorical guide, this piece provides insights and direction for the soul's journey towards divine love, spiritual awakening, and self-realization. The profound and symbolic narrative of Ras Leela continues to captivate and guide spiritual seekers, urging them to embark on a path of divine connection. It serves as a reminder to embrace the divine dance of cosmic love, fueling their pursuit of spiritual enlightenment.

Universal Love and Spiritual Union in the Ras Leela

With its profound significance, the Ras Leela is not just a performance but a majestic testament to a love that surpasses human comprehension. The portrayal of love in this depiction is one that knows no boundaries, is limitless, and encompasses all, extending its reach to every living being in the vast expanse of the universe.

Krishna's love for the Gopis, believed to be an expression of the divine, is not limited to earthly or worldly affection. This love can be described as celestial, embodying qualities of purity and selflessness, and serving as a mirror of the divine's love, which knows no bounds and is extended to all of creation.

Ras Leela, through its graceful movements and enchanting choreography, serves as a physical expression of cosmic love. The central concept it encompasses is that the divine is not distant or detached from the world, but rather actively and intimately engaged in the beautiful dance of creation, generously bestowing love and grace upon all beings.

The Ras Leela, a traditional dance in Indian culture, is not just a form of art but also a powerful symbol that represents the highest aspiration of spiritual seekers. This symbolic dance portrays the profound desire for the individual soul to merge and become one with the expansive universal consciousness. The representation of Krishna in this context is that of the universal consciousness, embodying the essence of all beings, whereas the Gopis symbolize the individual souls on a quest for divine union.

By means of the dance, the audience is able to witness the captivating portrayal of the soul's transformative path, evolving from a state of isolation to a harmonious connection with the divine essence. The significance of this is that it represents the soul's journey towards transformation, transitioning from the belief in being separate to the profound realization that it is eternally united with the divine.

When performing the Ras Leela dance, the dancers exude an overwhelming sense of ecstasy and joy, as the dance itself represents the incredible happiness that arises from the union of the soul and the divine. The experience is one of profound spiritual ecstasy, where the individual and the universal consciousness become indistinguishable from each other.

The love depicted in the Ras Leela transcends the limitations of the physical world. The love that we are referring to is not just any ordinary love, but rather a spiritual and sublime love that has the power to elevate the soul and free it from all earthly limitations, ultimately leading it towards the realization of the divine.

CHAPTER 10: RAS LEELA:

The Ras Leela is a beautiful display of how divine love embraces and includes everyone. Krishna's dance, where he gracefully partners with each Gopi, serves as a powerful symbol that divine love knows no boundaries and is accessible to every soul, disregarding any form of discrimination or bias.

The main focus of this event is to emphasize the belief that love is at the heart of everything that exists. The force that binds the universe together is not just a fundamental force, but also the essence that sustains creation and the ultimate reality that guides the soul towards enlightenment.

The union between Krishna and the Gopis in the Ras Leela is not just a simple encounter, but rather a transformative spiritual awakening that goes beyond the physical realm. It serves as a representation of the soul's understanding of its true essence and its connection to the divine.

Through the performance of the Ras Leela, participants aim to convey the idea that the ego and individual identity can be surpassed. When the Gopis engage in the dance with Krishna, a remarkable transformation occurs as their individual identities dissolve, serving as a powerful symbol of the soul's liberation from the limitations of the ego and its ultimate union with the divine.

Through the Ras Leela, one witnesses the powerful narrative of Bhakti and the transformative power of surrender. By fully surrendering and devoting oneself to the divine, one can witness the ultimate union and embrace the profound experience of divine love in all its magnificent forms.

Ras Leela in Spiritual Practices and Life

By integrating the lessons from the Ras Leela, individuals can deepen their spiritual practices and enhance their understanding. Their teachings emphasize the importance of individuals cultivating devotion, surrender, and a deep longing for union with the divine, as they believe it leads to spiritual growth.

By witnessing the Ras Leela, one can be motivated to embrace a life guided by love that knows no limits. By encouraging the embrace of love in its highest form, extending compassion and kindness to all beings, and recognizing the divine presence in everyone and everything, we can create a more harmonious and interconnected world.

The narrative implies that divine love transcends the realm of mystical experiences and is actually present in the mundane aspects of our everyday existence. By extending an invitation, individuals are prompted to actively search for and acknowledge the many different ways in which divine love is expressed in the world.

To summarize, the concept of "Universal Love and Spiritual Union" as depicted in the Ras Leela provides deep and meaningful understandings about the essence of divine love and the spiritual path towards union of the soul. The Ras Leela, an ethereal dance, surpasses the boundaries of its mythological background and symbolizes the universal love that unites the soul with the divine in a state of pure bliss. This particular instance serves as a powerful metaphor, symbolizing the intricate path of the soul's spiritual expedition and emphasizing the crucial role of devotion, surrender, and the recognition of oneness with the universal consciousness. The narrative serves as a powerful catalyst, inspiring individuals from all walks of life to wholeheartedly embrace and bask in the divine love that gracefully permeates every aspect of existence. Furthermore, it encourages individuals to diligently cultivate a profound and unbreakable connection with the divine, fostering a deep sense of spiritual union. Ultimately, the narrative beckons individuals to lead a life that is truly infused with cosmic love, allowing its transformative power to guide their every thought, action, and interaction. The Ras Leela, with its profound symbolism and enchanting choreography, stands as a timeless testament to the enduring pursuit of spiritual oneness and the profound impact of all-encompassing love.

Lessons on Devotion and Surrender from the Ras Leela

The way in which the Gopis react to Krishna's flute and subsequently participate in the Ras Leela showcases the epitome of devotion. The love they demonstrate for Krishna is steadfast and evident through their unwavering commitment to give up everything at a moment's notice, all in the name of divine love.

Their involvement in the Ras Leela extends far beyond simply being there in person. When the Gopis engage in their dance with Krishna, they symbolize the act of the soul relinquishing its ego, desires, and personal identity in order to unite with the divine.

The love that the Gopis have for Krishna goes beyond the limits of this world. This concept is not limited or restricted by societal norms or personal reservations. The love that exists between us is not only pure, but also selfless and all-consuming, serving as a powerful testament to the fact that true devotion can result in the ultimate surrender of oneself.

The Ras Leela is a symbol that represents the spiritual union that can be attained by surrendering oneself. The Gopis, while dancing with Krishna, undergo a profound experience of unity that leads to the dissolution of their individual identities. This signifies that genuine union with the divine is attainable solely through the act of wholeheartedly surrendering oneself in love.

The Ras Leela is a powerful teaching that demonstrates the ability to transcend attachments to the material world. By maintaining an unwavering focus on Krishna, the Gopis exhibit a remarkable sense of detachment from their mundane routines and worldly worries.

The story serves as a representation of a spiritual journey, showcasing the progression from the material world to the realm of the divine. The detachment from the material world that the Gopis display is not a deliberate act of renunciation, but rather a natural consequence of their profound devotion and love for Krishna.

The Ras Leela is a form of dance that beautifully showcases the joy and bliss that can be experienced through spiritual devotion. When the Gopis fully engage in the dance, they enter into a state of pure

CHAPTER 10: RAS LEELA: 249

bliss, indicating that genuine joy and fulfillment can be attained through spiritual endeavors rather than material acquisitions.

Another key aspect highlighted in the episode is the value of overcoming the ego. The Ras Leela, a divine dance performed by Lord Krishna and the Gopis, is a powerful symbol of the dissolution of the ego and the importance of selfless devotion and surrender in attaining spiritual growth and union with the divine.

The Ras Leela, a traditional dance performance, serves as a prime example of Bhakti Yoga, which is known as the path of devotion. The display of devotion and love towards the divine is a powerful method that can lead to the attainment of spiritual enlightenment and a union with the divine.

If you are someone who seeks spiritual enlightenment, the Ras Leela can offer you valuable insights and teachings. The teaching of this concept emphasizes that devotion and surrender, rather than being seen as signs of weakness, are actually strengths that can guide individuals towards spiritual liberation and enlightenment.

The Ras Leela not only showcases the beauty of devotion but also highlights the importance of divine grace in this sacred journey. The fact that Krishna accepts the love of the Gopis and reciprocates with them is a clear indication that divine grace plays a vital role in the journey of devotion.

By witnessing the Ras Leela, individuals are motivated to adopt a lifestyle characterized by unwavering devotion and surrender. The encouragement to incorporate these principles into one's daily life serves the purpose of fostering a more profound connection with the divine and transcending the constraints of the material world.

One of the main themes of the narrative is the encouragement and promotion of fostering an inner spiritual life. The implication is that the journey of devotion and surrender commences from within oneself, by fostering a personal bond with the divine that nourishes the soul and guides one towards spiritual contentment.

The Ras Leela imparts valuable lessons that can be applied to finding devotion in the actions we take every day. The core message behind this teaching is that by performing every action with love and a deep surrender to the divine, we can transform even the simplest tasks into acts of devotion.

In conclusion, the Ras Leela imparts valuable lessons on the importance of devotion and surrender, offering profound insights into one's spiritual journey. The Gopis' complete surrender in love, their ability to transcend worldly attachments, and the spiritual bliss they achieve by devoting themselves to Krishna, serve as a guiding example for living a life that revolves around divine love and spiritual union. The teachings presented here serve as an inspiration for individuals to embark on a journey of devotion, which ultimately leads to a life filled with profound spiritual depth, inner peace, and a sublime union with the divine. The Ras Leela transcends its status as a mere mythological story and takes on a greater significance.

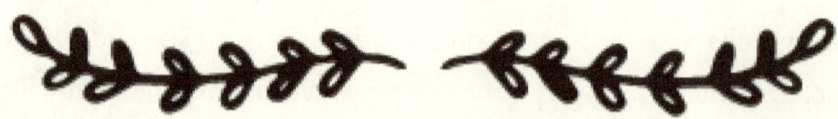

The Ecstasy of Spiritual Bliss in the Ras Leela

The Ras Leela, a traditional dance in India, is known for its ability to create a profound and overwhelming spiritual ecstasy among its participants. This ecstasy stems from the deep, unconditional love the Gopis feel for Krishna, which is reciprocated by him in the dance.

The Ras Leela is a sacred dance where the Gopis experience a transcendence of self, surrendering their individuality and fully embracing the ecstasy of divine love. The loss of self should not be seen as a negation of identity, but rather as a beautiful transformation into a higher state of being, where the soul experiences sheer ecstasy in the presence of the divine.

The state of extreme ecstasy that the Gopis experienced serves as a powerful symbol of the highest form of bliss that comes from being united with the divine. This state of profound spiritual fulfillment is characterized by the soul's experience of an indescribable joy and contentment that goes beyond the pleasures of the material world.

Through its enchanting performances, the Ras Leela transports spectators to a realm that exists beyond the limitations of the physical world. The dance has the remarkable ability to elevate those who partake in it to a transcendent state of consciousness, freeing them from the constraints and burdens of the physical realm.

Immerse yourself in the dance and discover a whole new world of higher consciousness that awaits you. By shedding light on the essence of spiritual awakening and realization, it reveals a state of consciousness in which the soul is enveloped in limitless joy and freedom.

Symbolizing the soul's quest for enlightenment, the Ras Leela is known for its ethereal nature. The representation of the soul's ascent from the mundane to the sublime is a symbolic journey that signifies the liberation from earthly constraints and the exploration of vast spiritual dimensions.

The Ras Leela is an experience that has the power to transform individuals through spiritual ecstasy. The profound impact of this transformation changes the Gopis at their very core, shifting their consciousness to a divine state and completely transforming their perception and comprehension of existence.

The Ras Leela, with its ecstatic movements and divine aura, has the power to awaken a heightened spiritual awareness within all those who partake in it. By serving as a catalyst, it facilitates a profound exploration of the self, the divine, and the intricate interplay between the two.

Through the Ras Leela, individuals are able to attain a state of spiritual bliss that aids in freeing them from their attachments to the material world. As the participants immerse themselves in divine ecstasy, they experience a profound transformation, witnessing the gradual fading of their attachments to the material world, as they come to a deep understanding of the transient nature of worldly desires.

The Ras Leela, with its spiritual ecstasy, holds a universal relevance that transcends boundaries. It symbolizes a model of spiritual encounter that individuals from different paths can strive for - a profound encounter in which love, happiness, and connection with the divine converge, resulting in a state of spiritual bliss.

Many people find inspiration for their spiritual practice in the Ras Leela. This demonstrates that the quest for spiritual bliss is not an unattainable objective, but rather a concrete encounter that can be realized by dedicating oneself, embracing love, and surrendering to the divine.

The Ras Leela, a traditional dance form, provides a blueprint for individuals to have profoundly joyful and spiritual encounters. These experiences go beyond just fleeting emotions; they are deep, profound states of consciousness that uplift the soul and offer profound insights into the true essence of reality.

To summarize, the Ras Leela's portrayal of spiritual ecstasy is a deep exploration that delves into the profound sense of joy that arises from being in union with the divine. Through the narrative of the Gopis, who completely lose themselves in divine love while dancing with Krishna, profound insights can be gained regarding the transformative power of spiritual ecstasy, the ability to transcend physical boundaries, and the attainment of an elevated level of consciousness. The experience of ecstasy has the power to transform individuals, resulting in personal growth, an awakening of spiritual consciousness, and liberation from attachments to worldly desires. The Ras Leela, a traditional dance performance, not only serves as a paradigm of spiritual experience but also acts as a profound inspiration for seekers who yearn to attain spiritual ecstasy through unwavering devotion, boundless love, and complete surrender. This stands as a powerful testament, showcasing the immense transformative power that spiritual bliss possesses, and highlighting the potential for every individual to partake in the euphoria of divine union.

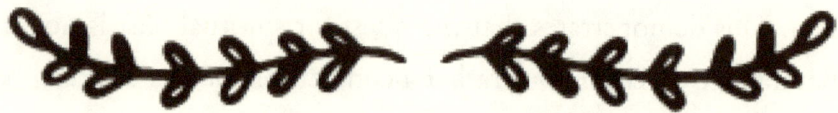

Integrating Ras Leela's Lessons into Life

Through the performance of the Ras Leela, the message of universal love and compassion is beautifully conveyed. The main goal of this is to inspire individuals to adopt a heart-centered approach to life, where they extend love and empathy to all beings, going beyond personal biases and selfish motives.

By engaging with the narrative, individuals are encouraged to foster empathy and kindness when interacting with others. By adopting a perspective of love, just like Krishna's affectionate gaze upon each Gopi, individuals can cultivate stronger bonds and enhance their comprehension of others.

By demonstrating acts of kindness, understanding, and support, individuals can incorporate the principles of universal love into their daily lives. The Ras Leela emphasizes that each interaction in life is a valuable opportunity for individuals to express and feel love and compassion.

The Ras Leela, a traditional dance form, serves as a powerful allegory that beautifully symbolizes the innate yearning of the soul to merge with the divine. By inspiring individuals, it encourages them to seek a deeper spiritual connection and highlights that the ultimate goal of human existence is this union.

Through the narrative, it becomes clear that the fundamental elements necessary for experiencing the divine presence are devotion, surrender, and love. The encouragement to adopt these qualities in one's spiritual practice is based on the belief that they play a vital role in paving the way to spiritual fulfillment and enlightenment.

By constantly keeping in mind the divine presence, one can easily incorporate the teachings of the Ras Leela into their daily life. The process of integration entails recognizing the presence of the divine in all facets of life and ensuring that our actions are in harmony with spiritual principles.

The Ras Leela is a representation that beautifully showcases the profound and transformative impact that divine love can have. The demonstration of love for the divine has the power to bring about profound transformations in an individual's life, enabling them to experience spiritual growth, attain inner peace, and ultimately achieve enlightenment.

The narrative effectively showcases how the power of divine love has the ability to triumph over the constraints of the ego. When individuals nurture their love for the divine, they gradually move beyond their ego-centered desires and behaviors, ultimately experiencing a more spiritually harmonious existence.

The Ras Leela, a traditional dance performance, not only entertains but also serves as a guiding force for individuals seeking spiritual growth and awakening. The idea conveyed is that by consistently dedicating oneself and displaying affection towards the divine, individuals have the potential to undergo profound personal changes that heighten their awareness and draw them nearer to spiritual realities.

Ras Leela's Teachings in Contemporary Context

The teachings of the Ras Leela have relevance and can be applied universally. Regardless of one's cultural or religious background, they provide valuable guidance on how to live a life that is filled with love, compassion, and spiritual awareness.

Given the fast-paced and often disconnected nature of today's world, the Ras Leela's emphasis on love, empathy, and spiritual connection holds a significant relevance. The purpose of this is to remind people to take a moment to slow down, connect on a deeper level with others, and nurture their spiritual life.

By incorporating the teachings from the Ras Leela, individuals can experience a positive transformation in their personal lives, which in turn can have a ripple effect on the larger community. Through the adoption of its teachings, individuals have the ability to actively participate in the creation of a society that is characterized by love, compassion, and spiritual awareness.

To sum up, by incorporating the teachings of the Ras Leela into our everyday lives, we can pave the way for a more meaningful, empathetic, and spiritually abundant way of being. In the Ras Leela, a traditional dance-drama, one can learn about the significance of universal love, the longing for divine union, and how personal transformation can be achieved through divine love. The teachings instill in individuals the importance of cultivating a heart that is brimming with love and empathy, guiding them to actively seek spiritual growth and a deep connection with the divine, and inspiring them to embrace and witness the profound and life-altering impact of divine love in all facets of their existence. The Ras Leela, an ancient dance form rich in profound symbolism and timeless wisdom, serves as a powerful source of inspiration and guidance for individuals who seek spiritual awakening, personal transformation, and a profound connection with the universal essence of love.

Conclusion: Embracing the Dance of Cosmic Love

The Ras Leela is a powerful representation of the highest form of love that exists, connecting humans with the divine. The depiction of love in this work goes beyond the ordinary, portraying a love that is all-encompassing, unconditional, and boundless. The love that exists between us is not limited to the physical plane; rather, it encompasses the spiritual realm, bringing about moments of ecstasy and facilitating spiritual enlightenment.

The symbolic significance of the dance between Krishna and the Gopis lies in its representation of the profound spiritual journey undertaken by the soul, leading towards awakening and ultimate union with the divine. Through the depiction, we can see how the soul, which is caught up in the material world, can ultimately reach a state of ecstatic unity with the universal consciousness by practicing devotion and cultivating love.

One of the key teachings of the Ras Leela is the significance of embracing universal love and empathy. By encouraging us to transcend our personal and selfish motives, this mindset enables us to extend our love and compassion to all beings, acknowledging and embracing the divine presence that resides within each and every one of us.

The narrative serves as an inspiration for those on a spiritual journey, urging them to aspire towards achieving a deep union with the divine. By dedicating oneself, surrendering completely, and embracing pure love, it is suggested that one can not only experience the divine presence but also achieve ultimate spiritual fulfillment in every aspect of life.

Through its portrayal of the Ras Leela, one can witness firsthand the immense power that divine love holds in shaping and changing individuals. The demonstration of love for the divine has the power to initiate deep personal transformation, foster spiritual growth, and ultimately lead to enlightenment.

Not only do the lessons of the Ras Leela pertain to ancient mythology, but they also have practical applications in modern-day existence. Their words and actions serve as a constant reminder for us to embrace a life filled with cosmic love, to approach each day with a mindset of spiritual love and devotion.

The narrative strongly emphasizes the importance of nurturing a spiritual perspective in our daily lives, wherein we intentionally infuse our everyday actions and interactions with love, compassion, and a profound comprehension of the divine orchestration at play.

By witnessing the Ras Leela, we are encouraged to actively engage in spiritual practices that cultivate a deep and meaningful bond with the divine. The integration of devotion, meditation, and mindfulness into our daily routines is vital as it underscores the significance of these practices in enriching our spiritual journey.

Regardless of one's cultural or religious background, the message of the Ras Leela resonates with all. The reason why it has a universal appeal is because it portrays love as a fundamental force that connects all beings and ultimately leads to spiritual unity.

The tale of the Ras Leela is not just a story, but a powerful source of inspiration that can guide us towards creating a world that is more harmonious and compassionate. This serves as a reminder that at the core of every spiritual tradition, there is a profound longing for love, unity, and a deep connection with the divine.

In summary, "Ras Leela: The Dance of Cosmic Love" encourages us to actively incorporate the cosmic dance of love and spirituality into our daily existence. The Ras Leela is portrayed as a profound allegory, which serves to deepen our comprehension of divine love, spiritual awakening, and the ecstatic union with the universal consciousness. The purpose of this narrative is to act as a guiding light, leading us towards embracing spiritual love and devotion, fostering universal compassion and empathy, and striving for the ultimate spiritual union with the divine. The Ras Leela, a sacred dance, serves as an eternal symbol that motivates and inspires us to partake in the celestial dance of boundless love, while embarking on a profound spiritual quest towards illumination and the harmonious merging with the collective consciousness of the universe.

Chapter Eleven

Chapter 11: Maharaja's Maturity

THE JOURNEY FROM PRINCE TO KING

Krishna's Early Years: The Playful Prince

In Vrindavan, Krishna's early life is filled with a succession of captivating stories that beautifully depict his divine nature and unparalleled charisma. Throughout his childhood, he experiences a multitude of miraculous events, engaging in playful acts and having profound interactions, which truly endear him to the hearts of the Vrindavan residents.

Even from a young age, Krishna exhibits qualities that are not only charming but also serve as clear indications of his divine essence. Don't be fooled by his seemingly ordinary playfulness; it is through this very facade that he unveils deep spiritual truths and cosmic principles.

Krishna, a youthful god, has become renowned for his extraordinary accomplishments, which encompass conquering malicious entities camouflaged as creatures and even exhibiting the entire universe within his own mouth. These acts, apart from being awe-inspiring, also communicate profound spiritual lessons that offer insights into reality and divinity.

Despite his young age, Krishna displays a profound understanding of life and spirituality that goes beyond what is expected of someone his age. Not only are his interactions with the people of Vrindavan playful, but they are also filled with wisdom and depth.

In every situation, be it his interactions with friends or his confrontations with adversaries, Krishna's actions reveal his inherent wisdom. His actions and words serve as a constant source of valuable lessons, particularly in matters of love, compassion, and the importance of duty.

The foundation of Krishna's later teachings can be traced back to his prior experiences in Vrindavan. The core principles of his spiritual and philosophical teachings in his later years are shaped by the values, insights, and understanding he cultivates during this period.

Krishna's childhood is filled with much mischief, ranging from sneaking away with butter to playing mischievous tricks on the Gopis. It is important to note that these acts should not be dismissed as mere child's play.

The spiritual significance of Krishna's playful acts, known as Leelas, cannot be overlooked. Krishna's actions serve as parables for spiritual teachings, whether it is about breaking free from material attachments, understanding the self, or experiencing unconditional love.

Through Krishna's interactions with the residents of Vrindavan, particularly his joyful and playful engagements with the Gopis, he establishes a profound and intimate bond with his devoted followers. The interactions that take place between devotees and the divine serve as a perfect example of how intimately involved the divine is in the lives of those who worship, as the divine responds to their devotion in incredibly personal and distinctive ways.

The early years of Krishna's life in Vrindavan serve as a guiding blueprint for those on the path of devotion, also known as Bhakti. Through his life, he shows that devotion encompasses more than just reverence; it also includes love, joy, and cultivating a personal relationship with the divine.

Although Krishna is divine, his life in Vrindavan is characterized by simplicity and humility. One can learn valuable lessons in compassion, humility, and positing a fulfilling life through his playful interactions.

Since a young age, Krishna has personified the concept of universal love. The deep affection he holds for the residents of Vrindavan, as well as the reciprocated love they have for him, vividly show the limitless and all-encompassing essence of divine love.

To conclude, Krishna's formative years spent in Vrindavan were characterized by divine play, valuable lessons, and delightful mischief, all of which provide deep insights into his spiritual path and teachings. Over the course of these years, a clear image has emerged of a deity who is not only approachable but also relatable and deeply connected with his devotees. Not only do the narratives of Krishna's early years and teenage hood entertain with their divine pranks, but they also impart profound wisdom on spirituality, devotion, and the true essence of life. Their encouragement extends to individuals, urging them to go beyond superficial observations, delve into the depths of life's experiences, and wholeheartedly embrace a journey of love, joy, and spiritual evolution. Krishna's early life, which was filled with charm, wisdom, and divine play, serves as a perpetual source of inspiration and guidance for seekers on their spiritual path, imparting timeless teachings on how to lead a life brimming with spiritual wisdom, boundless love, and unwavering devotion.

The Transition: From Prince to Leader

A Shift in Responsibilities

The transition in Krishna's life is marked by his journey from the pastoral beauty of Vrindavan to the politically charged realms of Mathura and Dwarka, which hold great significance. The shift being described in this statement is a transition from the innocence and simplicity of one's younger years to the intricacies and obligations that come with being an adult.

In both Mathura and Dwarka, Krishna is entrusted with significant responsibilities that require a high level of intelligence and competence. Throughout his journey, he undergoes a remarkable transformation, transitioning from a beloved village boy to a revered leader and king, who is entrusted with the immense responsibility of safeguarding the welfare and prosperity of his people and kingdom.

In this specific phase of Krishna's life, his ability to adapt to unfamiliar obstacles and circumstances was evident. Through his navigation of the intricacies of kingdom management, political alliances, and warfare, he shows his versatility and adeptness in handling a wide range of diverse and complex situations.

Leadership and Strategy

Krishna's role in both Mathura and Dwarka stands as evidence of his exceptional skills in governance, showcasing his ability to lead and govern effectively in different regions. His ability to implement well-thought-out policies and strategies plays a crucial role in maintaining the prosperity and stability of his domains, thus earning him the respect and admiration of his subjects.

Whether dealing with allies or adversaries, Krishna consistently shows his exceptional diplomatic skills. His approach to diplomacy is distinguished by a skillful balance of shrewdness, fairness, and foresight, which enables him to effectively establish alliances and prevent conflicts from arising.

Whether it be internal disputes or external threats, Krishna's strategic brilliance shines through in his involvement in various conflicts. He tackles complex situations using a combination of strength, well-thought-out strategies, and timely interventions.

Wisdom in Action

Krishna, being a mature leader, serves as a valuable source of guidance and mentorship for many individuals. His counsel shows an extensive comprehension of the intricacies of human nature, the complexities of societal dynamics, and the profound insights into spiritual truths.

A notable feature of Krishna's leadership style is his remarkable skill in harmonizing spiritual wisdom and practical governance, which sets him apart from others. Besides his authoritative leadership style, he also leads with compassion, righteousness, and a deep understanding of dharma, which is his sense of duty.

It is during this period of Krishna's life that his teachings, which would later be encapsulated in the Bhagavad Gita, are most prominently displayed. His counsel to Arjuna on the battlefield of Kurukshetra, where he skillfully merged spiritual enlightenment with practical advice, stands as a remarkable testament to his deep comprehension and invaluable guidance.

In closing, the journey of Krishna's transition from a prince to a leader is a remarkable tale that exemplifies personal growth, accountability, and sagacity. The journey that he embarked upon, starting from the lively streets of Vrindavan and leading him to the majestic thrones of Mathura and Dwarka, is not merely a physical expedition but a symbolic representation of his growth as a revered leader and trusted mentor. By skillfully navigating intricate political situations and combining it with his profound spiritual and philosophical understanding, he shows his versatile persona as a strategist, diplomat, and spiritual mentor. The particular phase of Krishna's life that is being discussed here serves as a profound inspiration for individuals, as it emphasizes the significance of being adaptable to new roles, wholeheartedly embracing responsibilities, and effectively using wisdom and compassion in the realm of leadership. Krishna's transition serves as a powerful reminder that every person can develop, transform, and take on more significant positions of authority and impact, all while remaining rooted in their spiritual and moral values.

The Role of Challenges in Personal Growth: Lord Krishna's Journey

Facing Adversities

During his younger days, Krishna encounters a multitude of demonic entities that were specifically dispatched by King Kamsa, intending to cause harm to him. Krishna faces a distinct challenge with each encounter, whether it is with Putana, Aghasura, or Bakasura, and he triumphs over them not only by using his divine power but also by employing his intelligence and strategic thinking.

Apart from the obvious physical confrontations, Krishna's stay in Vrindavan is defined by a multitude of other challenges. These challenges encompass safeguarding the villagers and their livestock from natural disasters, as well as navigating the intricate web of emotions and devotion displayed by the Gopis.

Learning from Experiences

The transition of Krishna from Vrindavan to Mathura, followed by his resettlement in Dwarka, exposes him to a whole new set of obstacles that he must navigate. Through his expertise in handling political intrigue, efficiently managing kingdom administration, and successfully leading battles against oppressive regimes, he shows his exceptional capabilities.

In the early encounters of Krishna with demonic forces, he not only engaged in physical battles but also gained valuable lessons about the true nature of evil, the immense power of righteousness, and the crucial importance of safeguarding dharma, which signifies duty and righteousness.

The experiences that he has in Vrindavan play a substantial role in the emotional and spiritual development of Krishna. Through his journey, he gains knowledge about the intricacies of human emotions, the profoundness of devotion, and the significance of cultivating strong relationships.

Overcoming and Learning from Adversities

As we delve into the cities of Mathura and Dwarka, we witness Krishna facing challenges that not only test his intellect but also present intricate ethical dilemmas. With great dedication, he hones his expertise in governance, diplomacy, and strategy, skillfully juggling the interests of his people while ensuring the preservation of peace and dharma.

Krishna's personal growth is influenced by each challenge he encounters, as they serve as catalysts for his development. Through their transformative powers, they not only shape him but also sharpen his abilities and enhance his comprehension of the intricate workings of the world.

When faced with adversities, Krishna stands out with his remarkable ability to respond with a perfect balance of compassion and justice. When faced with challenges, he consistently chooses solutions that not only uphold moral and ethical standards, but also show his capacity for empathy and understanding.

The challenges that Krishna faces and successfully overcomes play a crucial role in the development of his discernment and wisdom. His remarkable journey is a simple demonstration of how the combination of positive and negative experiences can affect an individual's personal and spiritual development.

The Evolution of a Divine Incarnation

The transformation of Krishna, from a playful child in Vrindavan to a wise and strategic leader in Mathura and Dwarka, serves as a clear illustration of his evolution. His multifaceted personality is shaped by the various challenges he faces in each phase of his life.

Krishna, throughout his entire life, exemplifies divine qualities that include compassion, wisdom, and an unwavering commitment to justice. The trials he faces along his journey serve as a platform for testing, refining, and ultimately showcasing the manifestation of these qualities.

The life of Krishna, which is filled with a multitude of experiences and valuable lessons learned from facing adversities, leaves a lasting and profound impact on the generations to come. His story, especially the teachings found in the Bhagavad Gita, serves as a significant source of guidance and inspiration for countless individuals around the world.

In summary, the story of Lord Krishna's personal growth revolves around the challenges he faces, which play a crucial role in shaping his transformation, learning, and evolution. Throughout his journey, which involves confronting supernatural entities and overseeing entire kingdoms, he undergoes a multitude of experiences that profoundly shape him into a revered figure and an astute leader. The life of Krishna vividly illustrates that when confronted with challenges, individuals who possess courage, wisdom, and discernment have the potential to undergo remarkable personal and spiritual development. Through his story, he inspires individuals to view challenges as valuable opportunities for personal growth, to extract valuable lessons from every experience, and to cultivate essential qualities like compassion, justice, and wisdom. Therefore, the narrative of Krishna's life serves as a timeless testament, highlighting the profound impact that challenges can have and emphasizing the inherent potential for growth and evolution in every individual's personal journey.

Krishna as a Mature Leader

Guidance and Mentorship

With his transition into a mature leader, Krishna emerges as a pivotal figure who plays a crucial role in guiding and mentoring others. The Mahabharata showcases his most significant mentorship, as he imparts invaluable wisdom to the Pandavas, with a particular focus on Arjuna.

The conversation between Krishna and Arjuna, which took place on the battlefield of Kurukshetra and is beautifully depicted in the Bhagavad Gita, perfectly showcases Krishna's role as a wise and guiding mentor. Through his discourse, he tackles the moral and spiritual dilemmas confronted by Arjuna, presenting profound and universally relevant perspectives.

Krishna's teachings encompass a wide range of topics, such as duty (dharma), righteousness, the nature of the soul, and the pathway to liberation. His wise counsel extends beyond the immediate context of the battlefield, offering timeless wisdom that can be applied in various situations.

Balancing Justice and Compassion

Krishna's leadership is truly remarkable as it effectively balances both justice and compassion. Despite frequently finding himself in challenging circumstances that demand tough choices, he consistently demonstrates a compassionate approach and a profound comprehension of what is morally just.

Krishna's unwavering commitment to dharma is a fundamental element of his leadership. Through his actions, he proves that true leadership extends beyond the mere exercise of power and encompasses the unwavering dedication to uphold moral and ethical values, especially when faced with difficult circumstances.

Despite his status as a powerful figure, Krishna consistently makes decisions that demonstrate his empathy and prioritize the greater good. Through his actions, he demonstrates that leadership is about comprehending the consequences of decisions on individuals and the community.

Inspiration for Future Generations

The inspiring journey of Krishna, from prince to king, and his significant role as a guide and mentor in the Mahabharata, have continued to captivate and motivate people for countless generations. The narrative of his life is not solely focused on his rise to power, but rather on the development of wisdom, responsibility, and enlightened leadership.

Krishna's life serves as a compelling example of how wisdom and responsibility form the cornerstone of effective leadership. By weaving together power, wisdom, and responsibility, his story serves as a testament to the potential of enlightened leadership.

Krishna's teachings and leadership style have not only become integral parts of spiritual and leadership discourses worldwide, but they have also greatly influenced and shaped the way individuals approach these subjects. Leaders in various fields can draw inspiration from his approach to leadership, which seamlessly blends strength with compassion and wisdom with action.

To sum up, Lord Krishna's portrayal as a mature leader provides deep understanding and valuable lessons on the subjects of leadership, mentorship, and spiritual guidance. The teachings found in the Bhagavad Gita, known for their profound philosophical insights and practical wisdom, remain an enduring source of inspiration and guidance. Krishna's exceptional skill in maintaining a delicate balance between justice and compassion, combined with his unwavering dedication to upholding dharma, establishes him as an enduring model of enlightened leadership. The progression he made from a charismatic prince to a sagacious ruler and guide encapsulates the values of developing wisdom, ethical duty, and empathetic leadership. Krishna's life serves as a guiding light for individuals who aspire to embody mature, responsible, and enlightened leadership in both their personal and professional endeavors.

Conclusion: Embracing Maturity and Wisdom

Krishna's Evolutionary Journey

The life story of Krishna serves as an extraordinary testament to the process of personal growth and the development of wisdom. The journey that he embarked on, starting from the playful antics in Vrindavan and continuing through the complex challenges he faced as a king in Mathura and Dwarka, truly demonstrates an exceptional evolution of character and understanding.

In every stage of his life, Krishna adeptly manages to strike a perfect equilibrium between his celestial nature and the range of human experiences he undergoes. The life he led is a powerful testament to the incredible potential that lies within every individual to grow, develop, and embrace greater wisdom and responsibility.

The Role of Challenges and Learning

The path that Krishna embarks on is filled with a multitude of challenges, and it is through overcoming these obstacles that he gains valuable insights and deepens his wisdom. Through a variety of experiences, including moments of joy and hardship, this individual's life exemplifies the significance of personal growth and the acquisition of leadership qualities.

By studying Krishna's story, we learn the importance of perceiving challenges as chances to develop and evolve. His remarkable ability to learn and grow from every situation, to adapt quickly to new circumstances, and to consistently make wise and informed decisions serves as an inspiring example of how one can embrace life's adversities as valuable opportunities for personal growth, maturity, and the acquisition of wisdom.

Leadership and Mentorship

Krishna, being a mature leader, demonstrates an exceptional ability to maintain a harmonious equilibrium between justice, compassion, and strategic acumen. The role that he played in guiding the Pandavas, particularly when considering the Bhagavad Gita, is a testament to his deep wisdom and comprehensive understanding of life's intricacies and the importance of fulfilling one's duty.

Krishna's mentorship is not limited to the battlefield of Kurukshetra; it extends to other areas as well. The teachings and counsel provided by him serve as a constant source of inspiration and guidance for individuals in both their personal and professional lives. They emphasize the significance of ethical leadership and the pursuit of spiritual growth.

Inspiration for Modern Times

Even in modern times, Krishna's life continues to be relevant and inspiring, transcending through the ages. The story he tells serves as a compelling reminder that every individual has the capacity to develop, to adopt wisdom, and to take charge with kindness and empathy.

By examining Krishna's journey, one can gain valuable insights into the specific qualities that contribute to being a highly effective and enlightened leader. The way he is able to handle complex situations, displaying empathy, foresight, and a profound understanding of human nature, sets a remarkable example for leaders and individuals alike.

Embracing Maturity and Wisdom

To conclude, "Maharaja's Maturity: The Journey from Prince to King" is an engaging narrative that effectively showcases the transformative voyage undertaken by Lord Krishna. This encapsulation of true maturity and wisdom offers invaluable lessons not only in personal growth but also in leadership and the journey towards enlightenment. The life story of Krishna serves as a source of inspiration, urging us to cultivate maturity in both our thoughts and actions, to actively pursue wisdom through our experiences, and to strive towards becoming leaders who effectively balance justice and compassion, as well as strategic acumen and ethical responsibility. The transformation of this playful prince into a wise king serves as a profound example of how every person has the capacity for growth and development, ultimately leading us to become responsible, empathetic, and successful leaders in both our personal and professional endeavors.

Chapter Twelve

Chapter 12: Divine Departure

Embracing Endings as New Beginnings

Krishna's Final Days: The Closing Chapter

The last moments of Krishna's life signify the conclusion of a momentous period in mythological history. The transition from the Dvapara Yuga to the Kali Yuga, which is characterized by a profound sense of change, signifies a cosmic shift in the universe's order during this period.

With Krishna's imminent departure from the mortal realm, one cannot help but sense a tangible atmosphere of contemplation and transformation. The moments leading up to Krishna's departure are not only moments of deep introspection for him, but also for all those who have been part of his journey.

Despite sadness, there is a prevailing atmosphere of serene acceptance that can be felt throughout Krishna's last days. The sense of tranquility present in his work is a direct reflection of his profound comprehension of life's impermanence and the perpetual cycle of birth and death.

The circumstances that surround Krishna's departure are characterized by a moment that is filled with deep irony and symbolism. Mistaking Krishna's foot for a deer, a hunter shoots an arrow, which ultimately becomes the means of his departure from the world.

Despite its mundane and accidental nature, the arrow holds significant metaphorical implications. By showcasing the unpredictability of life and the inevitability of death through the character of Krishna, this exemplifies the universal nature of these concepts that apply to both mortals and divine beings.

The seemingly insignificant cause of Krishna's departure signifies the ultimate conclusion of his divine play (Leela) on earth. This concept serves to emphasize the idea that even divine incarnations, within the broader context of the cosmic scheme, are bound by the laws that govern the material world.

In his last moments, Krishna showcases a remarkable and profound acceptance of the inevitable. The way he maintained his composure even when faced with death serves as a genuine reflection of the teachings he shared throughout his life, centered on the eternal nature of existence and the immortality of the soul.

Krishna's response to the series of events that led to his departure was a testament to his profound wisdom and comprehensive comprehension. Despite the circumstances, he maintains a sense of detachment and serenity, seeing his departure as simply another step in the never-ending cycle of life.

Through his last act, Krishna teaches others by leading through example. One can observe how he exemplifies the concept of facing the inevitable end of life's journey with both grace and understanding, acknowledging that death is simply a natural part of the continuum of existence.

With Krishna's departure, deep contemplations on the essence of life, the inevitability of death, and the everlasting nature of the soul come to the forefront. When considering this, it brings to mind the transient nature of the physical world and the eternal continuity of the soul.

Despite Krishna's imminent departure from the physical realm, his teachings and legacy persist and resonate deeply. His life and departure are profound symbols that remind us of the spiritual truths he embraced and passed on to others.

Rather than being seen as an end, Krishna's departure is regarded as a shift to a new form of existence. The belief in the soul's immortality and its spiritual journey extending beyond physical limitations is reaffirmed.

To sum up, the last days of Krishna and his eventual departure from this mortal realm serve as a perfect embodiment of the profound teachings he imparted on the subjects of life, death, and the everlasting essence of the soul. By calmly accepting what cannot be changed and leaving in a way that carries symbolic meaning, he provides deep understanding of the essence of life and the unending pattern of birth and demise. Krishna's last chapter is far more than just a wrapping up of his physical journey—it acts as a doorway that leads to a more profound comprehension of the spiritual path and the timeless continuum of existence. His life and departure can be seen as a guiding light, reminding us to approach life's transitions with wisdom and grace. We should remember that every ending is a necessary part of the eternal cycle of beginnings and continuations in the cosmic play of existence.

Embracing Change and Mortality

Understanding the Impermanence of Life

By leaving this world, Krishna emphasizes the impermanence that characterizes life. The culmination of his life, characterized by divine play, profound wisdom, and impactful leadership, is encapsulated in a singular moment that serves as the perfect embodiment of the inevitable nature of change and the impermanence of our physical existence.

The life and departure of Krishna serve as a lesson, highlighting the transient nature of everything in the material world, irrespective of its characteristics or importance. The recognition and acceptance of impermanence can serve as a catalyst for individuals to develop a deeper appreciation for the precious moments that life offers and to delve into a more profound exploration of the spiritual aspects of their being.

The journey of Krishna serves as a powerful example, demonstrating the importance of accepting and embracing the inevitable changes that accompany life, as they are crucial for one's personal and spiritual development. His acknowledgement and embrace of the inevitable end signifies his profound comprehension that change, whether it brings happiness or difficulties, is a fundamental aspect of the journey through life.

Mortality as a Natural Stage

The concept of mortality takes on a different meaning from Krishna's departure. Instead of being perceived as a dreaded or sorrowful conclusion, it is depicted as a seamless progression in the cycle of life, an unavoidable metamorphosis that every living creature must experience.

One of the main points the narrative highlights is the interconnectedness of life and death, emphasizing that they are two integral parts of the same cycle. With a life enriched by divine interventions and profound teachings, Krishna's eventual departure stands as a testament to the delicate equilibrium and interdependence of creation and dissolution in the cosmic cycle.

The way Krishna embraces the idea of mortality brings about a greater comprehension of the overall scope of existence. One of the main ideas behind this concept is to inspire people to perceive life as a component of a grand cosmic play, in which death is not seen as a finality, but as a passage into a new form of existence.

Preparation for Transition

The way Krishna handles his departure shows the significance of being ready for the changes that life brings. One of the key elements of living a meaningful life is the ability to embrace change, even when it involves the inevitable conclusion of our physical existence.

One of the valuable lessons we can learn from Krishna's life is that endings, be it the culmination of a phase, a relationship, or even life itself, are essential components of our personal journey. The moments of transition act as gateways that open up to fresh starts and different stages of existence.

In the narrative, there is a powerful encouragement to approach life with both acceptance and awareness of its transient nature. The presence of this awareness contributes to a more fulfilling and meaningful life, cultivating a greater comprehension of oneself, the surrounding world, and the profound spiritual nature of existence.

To summarize, the exploration of "Embracing Change and Mortality" from the perspective of Krishna's departure provides valuable insights into the importance of comprehending and embracing the transient nature of life and the inevitability of mortality. The outlook of this perspective is to view change and endings as natural and inevitable stages in the cycle of existence, rather than something to be feared. The life and departure of Krishna are powerful reminders for us to approach life's changes and transitions with wisdom, awareness, and acceptance. By presenting a detailed guide, this narrative aims to assist individuals in navigating life's inevitable transitions. It emphasizes the significance of incorporating an awareness of mortality and impermanence into one's approach to life. When individuals fully embrace the transient nature of existence, they can experience a more fulfilling life, where each moment is cherished and a profound connection to the spiritual journey that extends beyond the physical realm is established.

Legacy and Continuation

Enduring Teachings and Impact

Over the centuries, the timeless teachings of Krishna, particularly those beautifully expressed in the Bhagavad Gita, have proven their enduring significance. His profound teachings on duty, righteousness, devotion, and the nature of the self have been a source of guidance and solace for millions of individuals across the globe.

Krishna's life and teachings have had a deep and lasting impact on a multitude of spiritual practices and traditions around the world. Many spiritual paths have incorporated his teachings on Bhakti (devotion), Dharma (righteous duty), and meditation, recognizing them as fundamental elements.

Krishna's legacy goes beyond spirituality and leaves a profound impact on the realms of culture and philosophy. The life stories and teachings of this individual have served as a profound source of inspiration for various art forms, literature, music, dance, and philosophical discussions. This influence has shaped cultural expressions and fostered ethical understandings in many societies across the globe.

Krishna's teachings have a far-reaching influence that extends beyond the confines of India, both geographically and culturally. The messages of love, unity, and self-realization conveyed by him have resonated with people worldwide, contributing to ongoing philosophical and spiritual dialogues on a global scale. These messages have attracted a diverse range of individuals who are seeking greater significance and direction in their lives.

Life as a Series of Beginnings and Endings

The life story of Krishna serves as a powerful example of how life is an ongoing series of beginnings and endings. With every stage of his life, starting from his birth inside a prison and ending with his departure into a forest, represents a significant change, marking the end of one chapter and the start of another.

The departure of Krishna serves as a reminder of how temporary the physical world is, while also emphasizing the everlasting journey of the soul. It is important to recognize that every ending in life, whether filled with happiness or sadness, serves as a gateway to new beginnings and presents us with chances for personal growth and transformation.

The life of Krishna exemplifies the importance of embracing change as an integral part of our existence, encouraging us to do the same. The lesson it imparts is that instead of fearing endings, we should embrace them as natural progressions that open doors to new experiences and insights.

Continuation of the Divine Play

Understanding Krishna's life and departure hinges on recognizing the central role played by the concept of 'Leela', which encapsulates the idea of divine play. Within the vast cosmic tapestry, his existence on earth is perceived as a pivotal element in a greater narrative, where his deeds and teachings hold extraordinary importance in the universe's unfolding story.

Interpreting Krishna's departure from the earthly realm is not seen as a definitive conclusion, but as an ongoing continuation of the cosmic drama. This signifies a significant transition in his role, shifting from a mere physical presence to a more nuanced and spiritual influence that persists in guiding and inspiring.

The concept of Leela encompasses the continuous process of creation, preservation, and dissolution, with Krishna assuming an eternal role within it. Within the context of this cosmic cycle, his departure represents a transition that symbolizes the everlasting nature of divine influence and presence.

Conclusion: The Wisdom in Endings and New Beginnings

The final days of Krishna, along with his deliberate departure from the physical world, serve as a poignant reminder that life is a multifaceted and intricate voyage consisting of perpetual cycles. These cycles consist of a range of experiences, transitions, and transformations that mold our being. The eternal dance of existence encompasses every phase, ending, and new beginning, illustrating the interconnectedness of all things.

In the book "Divine Departure: Embracing Endings as New Beginnings," there are valuable lessons on gracefully accepting the temporary nature of life. Krishna's life is filled with divine interventions, profound teachings, and a departure that beautifully exemplifies wisdom. It serves as an invaluable guide for accepting the fleeting nature of our physical existence.

The narrative uses storytelling to inspire us to acknowledge and embrace the beauty and wisdom that accompanies life's conclusions. While Krishna's physical form comes to an end with his departure, it signifies a transition rather than a definite conclusion, ushering in a new phase of existence. This statement suggests that endings serve as important milestones that pave the way for new beginnings and promote a fresh perspective, rather than being definitive conclusions.

The story of Krishna emphasizes the concept that every conclusion paves the way for a new beginning. While his departure signifies the end of his time on Earth, it also opens doors for new spiritual manifestations and influences. This reminds us that in the complex cycle of life, endings and beginnings are interconnected, seamlessly transitioning from one to another in a continuous flow of existence.

Krishna's serene and contemplative manner of leaving and the profound influence he leaves in his wake inspire us, urging us to embrace life as a vivid tapestry woven with diverse encounters. Every experience, whether it ends or begins something, is crucial in shaping our complex lives, enriching our personal journey with depth and abundance.

When we contemplate Krishna's divine departure narrative, we are reminded of the significance of facing life's unavoidable changes with wisdom, comprehension, and openness. The message it teaches is that when we accept life's ups and downs gracefully and mindfully, we can peacefully and wisely navigate the path of life.

To sum up, Krishna's departure highlights the idea that life is a continuous cosmic drama. We should not view his passing as an end, but rather as a smooth transition into another dimension, an integral part of the eternal cycle that governs the vast universe, involving creation, preservation, and dissolution.

"Divine Departure: Embracing Endings as New Beginnings" is a profound exploration of the core of human existence, the captivating beauty inherent in the continuous cycles of life, and the inherent wisdom of fully embracing the certainty of change. This event is a joyful celebration of life's journey, highlighting the significance of embracing every phase and transition with understanding and acceptance. It serves as a reminder that every ending is the start of something new, as we participate in the everlasting and sacred drama of life.

Acknowledgements

In the journey of creating "Echoes of Krishna," I have been fortunate to receive the unwavering support and invaluable wisdom of many individuals whose contributions made this book a reality.

I am eternally grateful to my family, whose unwavering love and unwavering belief in my vision have been my unwavering source of strength and inspiration. My friends deserve recognition for their unwavering support and for being the sounding board for my endless stream of ideas.

I would like to express my deepest gratitude to the Lord Krishna and the mentors and teachers who have patiently guided me in unraveling the profound philosophies that lie at the heart of this book. I have valued their insights, as they have played a crucial role in shaping my thoughts and writings.

I would like to give a special shout out to the vibrant communities of Nepal and Toronto, whose presence has been a sanctuary and has broadened my perspective of the world and spirituality.

Finally, I want to express my sincere thanks to you, the reader, for taking this remarkable journey alongside me. Your engagement and reflections bring these words to life on these pages.

www.ingramcontent.com/pod-product-compliance
Lightning Source LLC
Chambersburg PA
CBHW031059080526
44587CB00011B/743